How To F Up Your Life

It's not what you think.

Written by: Cyndi Merritt

Copyright ©2025

Copyright ©2025, Cyndi Merritt

All rights reserved. No part of this publication may be reproduced, distributed and/or transmitted in any form or by any means, including photocopying, recording, or other electronic or mechanical methods, without the prior written permission of the publisher and/or author, except in the case of brief quotations embodied in critical reviews and certain other noncommercial uses permitted by copyright law.

Although the author and publisher have made every effort to ensure that the information in this book was correct at press time, the author and publisher do not assume and hereby disclaim any liability to any party for any loss, damage, or disruption caused by errors or omissions, whether such errors or omissions result from negligence, accident, or any other cause.

Adherence to all applicable laws and regulations, including international, federal, state and local governing professional licensing, business practices, advertising, and all other aspects of doing business in the US, Canada or any other jurisdiction is the sole responsibility of the reader and consumer.

Neither the author nor the publisher assumes any responsibility or liability whatsoever on behalf of the consumer or reader of this material. Any perceived slight of any individual or organization is purely unintentional and coincidental.

The resources in this book are provided for informational purposes only and should not be used to replace the specialized training and professional judgment of a category-specific trained professional.

Neither the author nor the publisher can be held responsible for the use of the information provided within this book. Please always consult a trained professional before making any decision regarding your life circumstances or those of others.

ISBN 978-1-7376870-6-1

**For my daughter, Stephanie.
God gave me the strength to survive,
and you are the reason I want to.**

How To F Up Your Life

The First Five Foundations

Page	
7	Foreword
9	Face: It's all about you.
19	Family, Friends and Your Future Mate
65	Finances Financial Vehicles Budgeting Income Insurance Investing Retirement Last Will and Testament
155	Fitness First Things First Mental Emotional Physical
211	Faith

Foreword

How to F Up Your Life

This book probably is not what you expected when you picked it up. It is not a guide to ruin your life. In fact, I hope it inspires you to set up your life for the most meaningful and rewarding future you can imagine. It is a broad-brush overview of things you should consider when making life choices. So, whether you're starting out or starting over, I hope this guide makes it easier for you to evaluate your personal goals and start the necessary steps to achieving them.

Each chapter focuses on one of the First Five Foundational pillars of life:
Face
Family, Friends, and Your Future Mate
Fitness
Finances
Faith
These are your **"F" foundations**, the pillars that help you start strong and stay steady. Because if you do not know where you are going, you will never know when you have arrived.

Start with the end in mind. You can read the book straight through, front to back, or jump to the chapters where you want help first. Wherever you begin, take notes, highlight, and most importantly, *implement*. Action creates momentum. Take small steps. You do not have to do everything at once. If you try, you will definitely feel overwhelmed. Give yourself time to understand the ideas, make a plan, practice, and then revisit the book when you are ready for your next steps.

Good luck. Now go **"F" up your life**, in the best possible way!

Disclaimer: The information contained in this book is for educational purposes and should not be considered professional advice in any specific category. Before making life changing decisions, consult with a qualified advisor in the appropriate field who can evaluate your personal circumstances and make recommendations based on your specific goals and needs.

Chapter One

Face

Face

Who You Are and Who You Want to Become

"Not everything that is faced can be changed, but nothing can be changed until it is faced." ~James Baldwin

Let's FACE it. It's all about you! Before you can build lasting relationships, choose a career, or find direction in life, you have to start with one simple but powerful question: *Who am I?*

Most people spend years chasing success, love, and approval — all without really knowing themselves. But when you take time to *face yourself* honestly, something incredible happens: clarity begins to form. You start to understand what you value, what drives you, and who you're becoming.

This chapter is about that discovery — not who others say you are, not the roles you play, but the authentic, unfiltered *you.*

1. Facing the Mirror

It's time to **face you** — really face you.

When you look in the mirror, what do you see? Not your clothes, not your hairstyle, not the version you post online, but the person behind the eyes.

Ask yourself out loud: **"Who am I?"**

Now, write down your answer. Don't rush it. Let whatever comes up, come up.

If your mind goes straight to "I'm a student," "I'm a football player," or "I'm a computer programmer," stop for a moment — those are *what* you do, not *who* you are. This reflection goes much deeper than labels, job titles, or social identities. It's about uncovering what's inside: your character, your beliefs, your values, and the way you treat others when no one's watching.

If you're unsure where to begin, ask a close friend or family member to describe you. Tell them to be honest — no sugarcoating. Their perception might surprise you.

What do people say about you?
"She's kind and dependable."
"He's funny and adventurous."
"She's always willing to help."
Or maybe, "He's always stressed," or "She can sure party."

This feedback isn't judgment — it's reflection. It shows you how you're showing up in the world. Do you like what you heard? Is there something you want to change? Do you like how you are perceived?

Self-Reflection Prompts

- What three words would others use to describe you?
- What three words would *you* use to describe yourself?
- Where do those lists match — and where do they differ?
- When you look in the mirror, do you *like* who you see?

This exercise is not about perfection; it's about awareness. You can't change or grow without understanding where you stand today. Sit with this for a while before you move on. Think about you.

2. Who You Want to Be

Once you've faced who you are, the next question naturally follows: **Who do you want to be?**

Life pulls you in a hundred directions — work, school, social media, friends, responsibilities. In all that noise, it's easy to lose your sense of self and drift toward what everyone else expects. But deep down, there's something steady and true: your **personal values.**

Values are the *inner compass* that quietly directs your choices, your relationships, and your reactions to life. They're not about achievement; they're about alignment.

When you live by your values, life feels congruent — what you believe matches how you behave. When you don't, you feel unsettled, anxious, or disconnected.

Action Steps

- Write down five people you admire. What traits do they share?
- Think about moments when you felt proud of yourself — what value was being honored?
- Think about moments when you felt disappointed — which value was being ignored or violated?

When you can answer those questions honestly, you're on your way to discovering who you want to be.

3. Discovering Your Core Values

Let's explore some core values that shape who you are and influence how you show up in the world. These aren't goals — they're guiding principles that help you live with purpose and integrity. Each one represents a piece of the foundation that supports your character and your choices. Use these as a springboard to discover your character or use them to set a goal you want to add to your life. Can you see yourself in these?

Accountability

Accountability is about owning your actions and their outcomes — both the wins and the mistakes. It's being honest when you fall short and dependable when others rely on you. People who practice accountability build trust, maturity, and self-respect. It's not about blame; it's about growth and taking responsibility.

Balance

Balance is about knowing when to push and when to pause. Life isn't meant to be lived in constant overdrive. True balance means recognizing that rest, relationships, and reflection are just as important as achievement. It's giving attention to your whole self — physical, emotional, social, and spiritual.

Compassion

Compassion isn't just about being nice. It's the willingness to understand others and extend kindness, even when it's inconvenient. It also means showing compassion toward yourself — speaking gently instead of harshly, especially in your mistakes. When compassion is a core value, it creates healing both within and around you.

Courage

Courage is not the absence of fear; it's the choice to move forward despite it. Whether it's setting boundaries, standing up for yourself, or chasing a dream that scares you, courage gives life to all your other values. Without it, they remain only good ideas.

Creativity

Creativity isn't just about art or music — it's about finding new ways to think, problem-solve, and express yourself. Creativity keeps life interesting. It allows you to see possibilities where others see problems, and to bring color, innovation, and originality into everyday moments.

Faith

Faith doesn't have to mean religion. It's a belief in something greater than yourself — maybe God, maybe the purpose behind life, maybe the simple trust that everything will work out. Faith gives you peace when answers are unclear and reminds you that even in uncertainty, there's meaning.

Freedom

Freedom looks different for everyone. For some, it's the ability to travel or make choices without asking permission. For others, it's emotional freedom — being able to express yourself honestly and live without masks. When you value freedom, you begin to shape your life around authenticity and truth.

Gratitude

Gratitude shifts your focus from what's missing to what's already good. It's the practice of noticing — the smile from a stranger, a warm meal, the chance to try again. Gratitude keeps your heart grounded and your mind centered on abundance rather than lack.

Growth

Growth is more than self-improvement; it's self-expansion. It's the choice to stay curious, to learn from mistakes, and to never let fear keep you small. Growth often happens in quiet ways — through reflection, discipline, or simply showing up one step better than yesterday.

Health

Health goes far beyond physical fitness. It's mental clarity, emotional balance, and energy for living. When you value health, you care for the body and mind that carry you through life. It's not perfection — it's respect for your own wellbeing so you can live fully.

Humility

Humility is quiet confidence — not thinking less of yourself, but thinking of yourself less. It's knowing you don't have all the answers, being open to feedback, and respecting others' strengths. Humility makes you teachable, kind, and real.

Integrity

Integrity means being the same person in private as you are in public. It's keeping your word, choosing honesty, and doing what's right even when it's inconvenient. Integrity builds trust and self-respect, two qualities that will serve you for a lifetime.

Perseverance

Perseverance is the ability to keep going when life gets difficult. It's finishing what you start and pushing through even when motivation fades. People who live with perseverance develop grit — that quiet, steady strength that keeps you moving toward your goals no matter how long it takes.

Respect

Respect means recognizing the worth in every person — including yourself. It's listening before speaking, honoring differences, and treating others as you want to be treated. Respect forms the foundation of strong relationships and healthy boundaries.

Service

Service means looking beyond yourself. It's helping others without expecting anything in return. Service could be as simple as holding a door or as big as dedicating your time to a cause. When service becomes a way of life, it fills you with purpose and leaves a trail of light wherever you go.

Work Ethic

Work Ethic isn't just about working harder or smarter. It's showing up consistently and doing your best. It's being responsible, reliable, and dependable — the kind of person others can count on. The value you bring to your studies, your job, or your personal goals is measured by your effort, integrity, and pride in what you do. True work ethic is giving your best in every situation and knowing that effort builds character as much as results.

Reflection Exercise: Discovering Your Own Values

1. **Reflect on Key Moments.** Think of times you felt proud, alive, or deeply fulfilled. What value was being honored? Then recall times you felt angry or disappointed — what value was being violated?
2. **Brainstorm Freely.** Write down 20–30 words that resonate with you (honesty, family, adventure, peace, growth, humor, etc.). Don't filter or judge.
3. **Group Similar Values.** Combine words that feel related (kindness, compassion, empathy = "Caring").

4. **Choose Your Top Five.** Ask: *If I had to live without this value, would life still feel meaningful?*
5. **Define Them.** Write a short sentence for each. Example:
    - Integrity: *I tell the truth even when it's hard.*
    - Family: *I invest time in those who matter most.*
    - Growth: *I learn from every experience.*
6. **Display Them.** Post your top five where you'll see them daily — your mirror, planner, or phone wallpaper. They'll serve as your daily compass.

At-a-Glance Summary: "Face"

Your Mirror Matters — See beyond titles; seek truth and awareness.
Define Who You Want to Be — Identify and honor your core values.
Discover Your Inner Compass — Reflect, refine, and display what matters most.
Live Your Truth — Let values guide choices and boundaries.
Keep Growing — Revisit beliefs, evolve, and live with purpose.

"Face" is about the most important relationship you'll ever have — the one with yourself.
When you know who you are, you stop chasing approval and start building a life that feels like home.

Favorite Points and Notes

Chapter Two

Family, Friends And Your Future Mate

Family, Friends and Your Future Mate

"A loving relationship is one in which the loved one is free to be himself to laugh with me but never at me; to cry with me but never because of me; to love life, to love himself, to love being loved. Such a relationship is based upon freedom and can never grow in a jealous heart."
~ Leo F. Buscaglia

This chapter is your guide to one of the most powerful forces in life — relationships. Every connection you make shapes who you are, who you'll become, and how you experience the world. The people you surround yourself with will influence your values, habits, and outlook in ways that are both subtle and profound. Family, friends, and your future mate are not just companions along the journey — they are mirrors, teachers, and guides. Through them, you'll learn lessons about integrity, compassion, patience, and love.

Life is an intricate web of relationships, each thread connecting to another, creating the network that supports and defines your life story. Some of these relationships will feel effortless, while others will challenge and stretch you. The key is to choose wisely, nurture the positive ones, and protect your well-being and your values in all of them.

We all share an innate desire to experience genuine connection — to be seen, heard, and valued for who we truly are. Yet so many people hold back, afraid of being misunderstood or hurt because of past experiences. But here's the truth: the effort to move beyond the surface is always worth it. Deep relationships — the kind built on honesty, trust, and mutual growth — have the power to transform your life. They strengthen your resilience, help you heal, and give you courage to face life's challenges with grace and confidence.

Make Sure You're Showing Up

Creating genuine connections starts with showing up — fully and intentionally. Be present. Listen without judgment. Notice the energy you bring into a room. People can feel when you're distracted or half-hearted, just as they can sense when you're fully engaged. Presence builds trust.

Everyone you meet is unique, with their own background, quirks, and perspectives. Embrace those differences. Meaningful relationships are not about changing people; they're about understanding and appreciating them. Being open, curious, and respectful allows room for genuine connection to grow.

Showing up also means letting others see *you*. Real relationships aren't built through perfection — they're built through honesty. Let your guard down. Share your story. Vulnerability is what transforms acquaintances into friends, and friendships into family. It's scary at times, but it's also the doorway to belonging.

Practice Honest Communication

Every strong relationship rests on honest, compassionate communication. Silence and unspoken resentment can quietly erode trust. The burden of unsaid words can weigh down a connection until it breaks. Speaking your truth, even when it's uncomfortable, is not confrontation — it's care. It shows respect for both yourself and the other person.

When you talk about what matters, set clear boundaries, and express appreciation openly, you create an atmosphere where understanding and growth can thrive. The fear of rejection or conflict may linger, but remember — you are stronger than your fear. Communication is how we build bridges, not walls.

Intentional Relationships Take Daily Effort

Strong connections aren't built overnight; they grow through consistent, intentional actions. Pay attention to how you show up for others:

- **When someone's upset**, give them space, but stay near enough to show you care.
- **When they succeed**, celebrate their wins as if they were your own.
- **When conflict arises**, don't rush to blame. Pause, listen, and work together toward understanding.
- **When small gestures appear**, notice them — gratitude strengthens every bond.

Relationships either deepen or fade based on the choices we make every day. Over time, your responses — your patience, empathy, and consistency — determine the strength of your bonds.

The Foundation of Trust

Every relationship will face challenges. What carries it through is trust — that unspoken belief that you can depend on one another. Trust grows when words and actions align. It takes time to build but can be lost in a moment of carelessness. Protect it by being reliable, honest, and kind.

A truly strong bond is one where both people feel safe, valued, and understood. You know they'll be there when you call, and they know the same of you. These are the connections that sustain you when life feels uncertain.

Presence and authenticity form the foundation of every genuine relationship. In moments of honesty and vulnerability, trust deepens, understanding expands, and real connection takes root.

Stay True to Yourself

While it's important to give in relationships, never lose sight of yourself in the process. Staying true to who you are means pursuing what genuinely makes you happy, not just what pleases others. When you live authentically, you naturally attract people who appreciate and love you for who you really are.

There's no need to pretend. There's no need to perform. The right people — family, friends, or a future partner — will connect with your real self, not your carefully crafted image. When you stay grounded in your values, life starts to feel aligned and effortless. Living in a way that contradicts your true nature is exhausting. Authenticity, by contrast, is freeing.

The world is vast and full of people who share your principles and energy. When you stand in your truth, you will draw those people toward you. Relationships built on authenticity will always outlast those built on performance.

Being Your Authentic Self

Authenticity begins with listening to your own voice. Self-reflection helps you identify what excites you, what frustrates you, and what you truly need to thrive. Ask yourself:

- What makes me feel alive?
- What drains my energy?
- What kind of people bring out the best in me?

Make time to explore your values and your personality. Know what you stand for, and let that knowledge guide your choices.

When you listen to the quiet voice within — your intuition — you find direction. Being authentic doesn't mean being rigid; it means being honest. It's about showing up as the truest version of yourself, even when it feels uncomfortable.

Authenticity liberates you. It gives you permission to stop chasing approval and start living intentionally. You don't need to twist yourself to fit into someone else's expectations. Instead, save your energy for what truly matters — the people and pursuits that reflect your purpose.

Practice Showing Up: As Yourself

Don't let judgments, comparisons, or limiting stories dictate how you live. The pressure to fit in can be strong, but remember — belonging isn't about blending in; it's about being accepted as you are. Slow down. Breathe. Stay connected to your values and your truth.

Showing up as your authentic self builds deeper, stronger relationships — the kind that nourish you rather than drain you. Be open, compassionate, and intentional. Listen deeply, love honestly, and forgive generously. These are the practices that keep connections alive. When you live this way, you don't just build relationships — you build a life filled with meaning.

Favorite Points and Notes

Family: Your First Classroom of Life

Let's start by talking about something that probably shapes more of your life than you even realize: your family. Now, I don't mean just the people you live with, although that's part of it. I mean the whole network: parents, siblings, grandparents, step-relatives, aunts, uncles, cousins—anyone who's part of your life because of who you are, and anyone who influences you, whether by choice or circumstance

Family is your first classroom. It's where you learn how to love, how to argue without breaking something (sometimes literally), how to respect others, and how to figure out your own role in the world. And I want you to know this right away: the type of family you were born into doesn't define you, it's what you do with it that counts.

Understanding the Family You Have

First, let's get real. Families come in all shapes and sizes. Some of you have the classic "mom, dad, two kids" setup, with a rhythm that feels predictable and safe. Some of you have a single parent working endless hours just to make ends meet, and maybe you've had to grow up faster than you expected. Others live in blended families with step-siblings or step-parents, trying to find your place in a group that wasn't chosen but that you need to navigate anyway. And some of you have grandparents, aunts, or uncles who raised you or who have become your main source of guidance and love.

Here's the thing: no matter your situation, you have a role. And understanding your role is your first step toward becoming someone you can respect.

- **Firstborns**: You often feel pressure to set an example. It can feel heavy, but it's also a chance to develop leadership and responsibility early. Think of yourself as a trailblazer, paving a path for those who come after you.

- **Middle children**: Sometimes you feel invisible, stuck between the overachiever and the baby of the family. But this spot teaches negotiation, compromise, and empathy. You learn how to mediate conflicts and see both sides of a story.
- **Youngest children:** People might underestimate you or treat you like the baby forever. Use that to your advantage. Develop independence, observational skills, and creativity. You can see how things work from a fresh perspective.
- **Only children**: Independence is your strength, but you need to stay socially engaged and practice collaboration outside the family.
- **Stepchildren**: It's complicated, I know. Feeling accepted and understanding your new family dynamic takes patience. But by being open, communicative, and willing to listen, you can carve out a place of significance.

No matter where you fit, your actions, attitude, and willingness to contribute define how you're shaping your family environment.

Family Values: The Real Backbone

Let's talk values: honesty, respect, responsibility, kindness, empathy, and perseverance. These are not just words to hear once and forget. They are habits you cultivate, and the earlier you do, the stronger your foundation will be.

- **Honesty**: It builds trust. When you tell the truth, even when it's uncomfortable, people learn to rely on you. That kind of trust is priceless, not just in family, but everywhere.

- **Respect**: It's more than saying "please" and "thank you." It's about listening, honoring boundaries, and understanding that everyone has their own struggles.
- **Responsibility:** Taking ownership of your chores, mistakes, and commitments shows you are someone people can count on.

- **Kindness and Empathy:** Understanding other people's feelings—parents, siblings, even those cousins who push your buttons—teaches compassion.
- **Perseverance:** Watching a parent work hard, seeing a sibling overcome setbacks, or observing a grandparent persevere teaches resilience. You absorb these lessons, even if they don't feel obvious at first.

These aren't just family lessons, they are life lessons. Mastering them now makes you someone who thrives in friendships, school, work, and, eventually, romantic relationships.

Roles Within the Family

Now, let's get practical. Every family has a hierarchy; it's not about superiority—it's about function. Each person contributes, and each role matters.

- **Parents**: They provide guidance, protection, and care. Sometimes that guidance feels strict or inconvenient, but it's often rooted in love. Their actions, words, and examples teach more than you realize.

- **Siblings:** They're your first peers. You learn compromise, cooperation, and resilience. You argue, laugh, and sometimes fight with each other, but these interactions teach you how to handle real-world relationships.
- **You**: Your position, whether as oldest, middle, youngest, only child, or stepchild doesn't define your value. What matters is how you show up, how you contribute, and how you uphold your family's values. Even small acts—like helping a sibling with homework, doing chores without being asked, or offering a listening ear to a parent—add up to a strong, reliable, and respected presence in the family.

Grandparents: Your Hidden Treasure

Grandparents are often undervalued in our fast-moving culture, but their stories and experiences are a goldmine. Spending time with them is beneficial for both of you.

- **For you**: Their stories of triumphs, mistakes, and lessons learned will give you great perspective on life. They show you how to navigate challenges and decisions that you haven't even faced yet.

- **For them**: You give them significance. They see that their lives mattered and that their wisdom carries on.

Ask them questions. Listen carefully. Share your life with them. These conversations are investments in your understanding of life and in their sense of purpose.

Toxic Family Members: Setting Boundaries

Of course, not every family member will lift you up; some could beat you down. Some may be struggling with self-harm or addiction; others may be toxic toward you. They may have destructive habits, struggle with addiction, behave irresponsibly, or display chronic negativity. Or worse, they might be abusive—physically, mentally, or emotionally—to you or someone else in the family.

That's tough to accept because, well, they're family too. But being related by blood doesn't give someone the right to cause pain. Here's the truth: it's not only okay—it's imperative and right—to set boundaries. You can care for someone without letting their poor choices damage your life.

There may come a time when you can no longer tolerate a family member's actions and you must make the hard decision to protect yourself and cut them off entirely. It can be a hard decision, because you might love them. If you've been exposed to toxicity for a long time, it can cloud your own judgment and make the behavior seem normal. Kind of the "you can't see the forest for the trees" effect.

Don't let yourself become blind to bad behavior, and don't tolerate or make excuses for a toxic person. If you read the foreword of this book, you know I come from a very toxic long-term relationship, so I share my firsthand experience of the impact and the time recovery can take. Protect yourself. It's hard, but you'll be better off in the long run.

- **Empathy without tolerance**: Understand their struggles but do NOT excuse their bad behavior.

- **Protection:** Prioritize your own emotional, mental, physical, and moral health. That's not selfish. You don't need to feel guilty. Do what's best for you.

- **Preparation:** If you must continue interacting with this person—for example, at holidays, weddings, or family events—set clear boundaries in advance. Know what you'll tolerate, and stick to it. This isn't about being cold; it's about survival, growth, and maintaining the principles your family should teach you.

Reflection and Action

Take a moment and think:

1. Am I contributing positively to my family?
2. Do I listen to and learn from my parents and siblings?
3. Am I actively engaging with grandparents or elders in my life?
4. Are there family members whose influence I need to limit for my well-being?

Write these reflections down. Set small, actionable goals. Maybe it's spending fifteen minutes with your grandparents each week, helping a sibling with chores, or saying "thank you" more often to your parents. These small acts shape character and strengthen family bonds.

Lifelong Impact of the Family

Here's the truth: your family shapes not just who you are today, but who you will become tomorrow. Every lesson learned, every boundary established, every effort to engage positively builds a foundation that influences friendships, professional life, and romantic relationships. By embracing your role, honoring family principles, and navigating challenges with integrity, you are equipping yourself to step into the world as someone grounded, resilient, and compassionate.

Family is your first teacher, and the lessons last a lifetime. Pay attention, participate actively, and take every opportunity to learn and grow. Your engagement, your integrity, and your willingness to contribute positively will determine the person you become and the life you build.

Note on Safety: If you or someone you love is experiencing abuse, neglect, or violence, please seek help. Reach out to trusted adults, local resources, or crisis hotlines. No one should face these challenges alone, and help is available.

Favorite Points and Notes

Chosen Relationships: The Sphere Around You

Alright, now that we've talked about family, the people you're born into, let's take a look at the relationships you get to choose.

Family is given. You didn't choose it. But life offers relationships you do choose: friends, mentors, coaches, teachers, pastors, and eventually a future partner. And here's a principle that's worth remembering: ***"You are the average of the five people you spend the most time with."*** Let me tell you, it's true!

Think about it: the way your closest friends think, the way your mentors act, the values your coaches reinforce, they all influence your behavior, your choices, and even your self-image. Choose these people wisely.

I say people, but you may have made relationships a priority with video games or television, or social media. These non-humans influence you too. Are you spending more time with those devices than with people? Read that quote again and insert the equipment influence: ***"You are the average of the five device substitutes you spend the most time with."*** That could be frightening.

Your inherited relationships, family, gives you your first lessons. Your chosen relationships build on that foundation. Surround yourself with people who uplift, inspire, and reflect the values you want to maintain. The wrong influences can subtly steer you off course, while the right ones reinforce your growth, character, and aspirations.

This part of your life is fascinating because it's where you start to shape your own world in ways that go beyond your household. Your friends, mentors, teachers, pastors, coaches, and even co-workers all play a role in shaping your habits, mindset, and overall trajectory. And here's the exciting part: you actually get to decide who these people are. So take an honest look at who or what you're allowing to influence and shape you.

Friends: The People Who Shape Your Life

Let's have a real talk about friends. Think about the people you spend the most time with outside your family—your peers, classmates, teammates, neighbors, or anyone who regularly crosses your path. At first, these relationships might feel casual, but they influence you more than you realize. The friends you choose can shape your character, habits, decisions, and even your future.

Friendship isn't just about sharing laughs or having fun; it's about building connections that challenge you, support you, and help you grow into the person you're meant to become. Some friends lift you up, while others may hold you back, and sometimes it takes reflection and experience to see the difference. That's why learning to choose, maintain, and evaluate friendships is one of the most important skills in young adulthood.

Why Friends Matter

Here we are again with that phrase: ***"You are the average of the five people you spend the most time with."*** It's not just a cliché—it's true. Friends influence how you think, act, and see the world.

If your friends prioritize partying, staying up late, or making impulsive decisions, you're more likely to adopt those habits. On the flip side, friends who volunteer, work hard, study diligently, or engage in meaningful activities encourage similar behaviors in you. Friends don't just reflect who you are, they shape the person you're becoming.

Influence isn't always obvious; even subtle behaviors, like how a friend talks about success or handles setbacks, will you teach lessons. Becoming conscious of these patterns gives you the power to choose friends who positively shape your life.

Identifying Positive Influences

Not all friends are created equal, and part of growing is learning to distinguish between those who support your growth and those who hinder it. Here are some qualities to look for:

- **Supportive**: True friends celebrate your successes and encourage you when you're struggling. They don't compete with you in unhealthy ways; they lift you up.
- **Trustworthy**: You should feel safe sharing your thoughts, goals, and struggles without fear that they'll betray you or gossip about you.
- **Aligned Values**: Friends who share your morals and principles reinforce behaviors you want to cultivate. These relationships help maintain your sense of integrity.
- **Positive Influence**: A friend may not be perfect, but they push you toward growth rather than dragging you down.

Think about someone in your life who inspires you to be better. What is it about their behavior, attitude, or perspective that you admire? That's the kind of friend you want more of.

Now think about someone who you regularly question their choices. Who do you need to distance or even eliminate interaction within your life?

Use them both as a mirror. Who are you reflecting? Who do you want to be more like? Let's look closer at those questionable friends.

Recognizing Toxic Friendships

Like toxic Family members, not every friendship is healthy, and recognizing toxic relationships is crucial. They may be easier to distance yourself from if needed, but it's still hard. Recognize that your toxic friends may:

- Spread negativity, criticism, or gossip
- Encourage poor habits like excessive partying or substance use
- Disrespect boundaries or undermine confidence
- Focus on themselves instead of supporting you
- Don't follow through on commitments, lie or cheat

Here's the hard truth: It's okay to distance yourself from people who consistently drain your energy. Setting boundaries isn't mean; it's self-preservation and staying true to your values. Sometimes you may feel guilty, especially with long-term friends. That's normal. You can care about someone while protecting your own growth and mental health. Once you recognize toxic behavior, you can see the influence your friends have more clearly. It's impossible to thrive if your inner circle of close friends is filled with negativity, chaos or self-destruction.

If this is ringing true, re-read the Toxic Family member section. Friends can certainly be like family, you love them and want what's best for them, but you do need to put your own self preservation first, no matter how hard that may be.

The Subtle Power of Friendship

Friends have an invisible power over us. They shape our habits, influence our decisions, and can even affect our emotional well-being. Let me give you an example. Imagine you have a friend who is always late, disorganized, and dismissive of responsibilities. Over time, their habits may start to influence you, even unconsciously. You might find yourself rushing, procrastinating, or lowering your standards without realizing it.

Conversely, having a friend who is disciplined, positive, and motivated can elevate you. Their behavior sets a standard, encourages accountability, and inspires you to match their effort. This is why being intentional about your friendships matters, it's a choice that affects your growth in ways you may not even notice yet. "All boats rise (or lower) together".

Building Trust

Trust is the cornerstone of strong friendships. Without it, relationships are shallow. A trustworthy friend respects your vulnerability, supports you when you stumble, and earns your confidence over time.

- **Trust develops over time**: It's earned, not given automatically. Observe how your friends handle challenges, whether they respect confidentiality, and how they respond to conflicts.

- **Mutual effort matters**: Strong friendships require reciprocity, that freely and happily given "give-and-take". Both friends need to give, listen, and support each other consistently.

Investing time and energy into friendships that demonstrate trustworthiness ensures that you have relationships built on stability, reliability, and mutual respect.

Shared Experiences Strengthen Bonds

Friendship isn't just about proximity; friendships thrive on shared experiences. Doing meaningful activities together strengthens trust, builds camaraderie, and creates memories that anchor relationships.

- **Volunteering**: Working together at a community shelter or charity event teaches teamwork, empathy, and compassion.

- **Sports and Recreation**: Team activities develop discipline, cooperation, and healthy competition.

- **Creative Projects or Clubs**: Engaging in music, inspiring books, art, debate, or other clubs foster collaboration, patience, and communication.

These experiences aren't just fun, they're foundational for long-lasting friendships. They teach you how to work with others, handle challenges, and celebrate achievements together.

Balancing Fun and Growth

I know, sometimes friendships can feel all about having fun. But here's the thing: real friends don't just entertain you, they challenge you. They push you to be better, hold you accountable, and encourage you to reach your potential.

- **Be intentional**: Ask yourself whether your interactions inspire growth or simply provide distraction.

- **Communicate openly**: Talk about your goals, values, and boundaries. True friends will respect and identify with them.

- **Reflect often**: Periodically assess your friendships and ask whether they align with the person you want to become.

The best friendships strike a balance between fun, support, and personal growth.

Ending Friendships When Necessary

Sometimes friendships need to end. Consistent disrespect, destructive habits, or lack of investment are valid reasons. Ending a friendship doesn't make you a bad person, it shows your intentionality about your growth. You may need to end the relationship, reduce time spent with someone or it may even include those non-human friends! Devices can become substitutes for the lack of friends. You may need to reduce time spent with addictive devices, games, or social media that reinforce negative patterns thereby making room and time to find real relationships.

Who or what is impacting you negatively?

- **Approach with respect**: You can step back without hostility.

- **Protect your values**: Remember why you're making the decision; it's about your integrity and future.

- **Reflect on lessons learned**: Every friendship teaches something, even if it doesn't last forever. Be grateful for what you've learned.

Ending a friendship can be difficult emotionally, but essential to protect your time, energy, and your life values.

Reflection Questions

1. Who are the five people you spend the most time with outside your family? Honestly look at those devices too.
2. Do they inspire your growth, or do they encourage habits that hold you back?
3. Which friendships need boundaries or closure? Take action.
4. What steps can you take to strengthen relationships with positive influences?
5. How can you engage in shared activities that deepen friendships?
6. How can you be a better friend to someone?

Identifying these people and writing these answers down will help you approach your friendships intentionally rather than letting them happen by chance.

Other Friends and Acquaintances

Now let's talk about all those other friends and acquaintances. Some friendships you choose; others are thrust upon you. In any case, they all influence your life and your growth.

Ancillary relationships may not come with the unconditional bond of family, or the close connection of your "best friend", but they can be just as powerful. Sometimes they can be even more so, impacting and shaping who you become. The beauty here is choice. You get to decide who enters your inner circle, whose advice you take seriously, and whose behavior you emulate.

Mentors and Role Models

Mentors are people who intentionally guide you. They're often older, wiser, and more experienced, but they don't have to be perfect. Their main job is to challenge you, push growth, and share lessons from successes and mistakes. Include them among the five people you spend the most time with—they'll help you grow.

Role models may be observed rather than interacted with. They demonstrate behaviors or achievements to emulate—teachers, coaches, public figures, or even historical icons. You can read their works, listen to podcasts, watch videos, or meet them if possible. Look for values you admire: integrity, respect, and purpose.

Both Mentors and Role Models demonstrate a standard of behavior or achievement you want to emulate. Maybe it's a teacher who always goes above and beyond for students, or a coach who shows persistence and fairness in every decision. It could even be a motivational speaker or a person of prominence like a celebrity, musician or political figure. They might even be long deceased but they inspire you by the words or impact they've left behind them! The point is you get to choose, follow and emulate.

Here's the thing: Mentors and Role Models aren't just there to give advice, they're there to show you what's possible when someone lives intentionally. Look for people whose values align with yours or values you are striving to achieve. If they live with integrity, respect, and purpose, that's someone worth learning from.

- **Practical Tip**: Identify one or two mentors in school, church, or community. Reach out, ask questions, observe their problem-solving, look at where they've come from and how they've achieved their goals. Respectfully appreciate their guidance and always be respectful of their valuable time.

Teachers and Coaches

Teachers and Coaches are a special type of relationship because they guide you in specific areas like academics, sports, arts, music or other disciplines. But their influence often reaches far beyond their subject matter.

Teachers: A great teacher models curiosity, discipline, and the love of learning. They inspire you to think critically, explore new ideas, and challenge you. Even if a subject isn't your favorite, pay attention to how they engage, how they set standards, and how they expect you to rise to them. You may not think you'll use a particular subject matter later in life, but that may surprise you! I use geometry a lot more than I ever thought I would! Great Teachers and

Professors will teach you HOW to think, not WHAT to think. They will encourage you to broaden your mind, make you think and ask questions and instill in you the desire to become a lifelong learner. There will be one or two teachers, more if you're lucky, you'll remember for the rest of your life. Theirs is the impact and encouragement that helps shape you and your future.

Coaches: Coaches don't just teach skills; they teach discipline, teamwork, resilience, and mental toughness. The lessons you learn on the field often carry over into other areas of life. If you respect a coach, listen closely, they often see potential in you that you don't see in yourself yet. As you evolve in your life, you should have multiple coaches. Your Coaches are not just in school or sports but will be in various areas where you want or need accountability. One may be there to improve your golf swing but another may be there to stretch your business goals. A great Coach will always challenge you to be better, try harder and do more than you think you can.

Pastors and Spiritual Leaders

If you are part of a faith community, your spiritual leaders can be incredibly influential. They serve as moral compasses teaching values like integrity, compassion, service, and humility.

Attend services regularly, observe leaders who live with purpose and serve others. This can be enlightening. They show you what it looks like to make choices guided by principle, rather than convenience or popularity.

- **Practical Tip**: Engage intentionally. Ask questions. Volunteer. Take note of the qualities you admire in these leaders. Over time, these lessons become part of your own moral framework.

Co-Workers, Bosses and Professional Connections

As you work or volunteer, co-workers, bosses and professional mentors become another layer of influence. The habits, ethics, and attitudes of your colleagues will shape your own approach to responsibility, teamwork, and career development. Be conscious of your work environment and adopt habits that serve your goals.

Evaluating Influence: Positive vs. Negative

Not everyone you meet will be ideal. Some teachers or coaches might seem unfair, some leaders may falter, and some bosses may be difficult.

Imagine working with someone who consistently shows up late, cuts corners, is rude with customers or spreads negativity. If you adopt their behavior, it will hurt your growth. On the other hand, worshiping alongside someone steadfast, diligent, creative, and respectful can inspire you to elevate your own standards.

Always be conscious of the culture you immerse yourself in. The lessons you learn from these relationships, about discipline, collaboration, and communication will carry into every area of your life. Good or bad, learn from these relationships but remember: their shortcomings don't define you. You get to decide how much influence they have over your mindset. Take what you like and leave the rest.

- **Positive influences:** These people encourage growth, challenge you to improve, and model behavior you want

to emulate. They celebrate your successes, offer guidance when you stumble, and reinforce your values.
- **Negative influences:** These individuals may spread cynicism, encourage poor habits, or undermine your confidence. While they might be unavoidable in some situations, such as a required class or workplace, you need to set boundaries and limit their influence. Remember: being polite or friendly doesn't mean you have to adopt someone's negative habits or allow them to drain your energy. Protect your values, your time, and your mental health.

Building Your Circle Intentionally

Now let's get practical. Here's how to build a circle of ancillary relationships that supports your growth:

- **Identify role models:** Who inspires you? Who demonstrates values you want to embody? Observe their behaviors and learn.

- **Seek mentorship**: Don't wait for mentors to appear magically. Take initiative. Reach out, ask questions, and show initiative. Mentors are often willing to guide you if you demonstrate commitment and respect.

- **Evaluate regularly**: Every few months, reflect on your circle. Are these relationships helping you grow, or are they holding you back? Adjust accordingly.

- **Engage actively**: Attend events, volunteer, or participate in activities that expose you to positive influences. Passive observation is helpful, but active engagement accelerates growth.

- **Set boundaries**: Know when to step back from relationships that drain or mislead you. Limiting contact with negative influences is not selfish, it's self-preservation and is strategic for your personal development.

Practical Tip: Here's the key question you need to ask yourself constantly: *Is this person lifting me up or holding me back?*

Reflection Questions for You

1. Who are the people you spend the most time with outside your family?
2. Are they helping you become the person you want to be? Who deserves more time, and who less?
3. Who could be a mentor in your life, and what steps can you take to learn from them?
4. How do your teachers, coaches, or spiritual leaders influence your values and habits?
5. Which relationships need boundaries to protect your growth?

Reflect often especially when people move in or out of your life, when your job changes or your class schedule changes. Revisiting these questions can help you stay intentional about the people you allow to influence you.

Take this responsibility seriously. Surround yourself with people who inspire you, challenge you, and lift you higher. Learn from those who live intentionally and step away from those who drain or mislead you. These relationships, carefully selected, will guide your path, reinforce your values, and help you grow into the person you're capable of becoming.

Lifelong Perspective on Friendships

Friendships are more than companionship; they are mirrors, teachers, and motivators. The people you choose now influence your adulthood, career, character, and even your future family. Strong friendships teach trust, loyalty, empathy, and resilience. They provide a network of support, encouragement, and honest feedback when you need it most.

Remember: friendships require effort, but the effort is worth it. Choose friends and the people who surround you with those who elevate you. Engage actively in these relationships, and step away from those who drain you. Your social circle is a powerful tool in shaping the person you're becoming. Your circle is your tribe, your village, and your sphere of influence. Create it wisely—use it wisely.

Favorite Points and Notes

Future Mate
Dating and Finding a Lifelong Partner

Lastly, let's dive into one of the most important areas of your life: the relationship that could—and if done right, should—last a lifetime. Even considering current cultural norms, I want to advocate dating with the intention of finding your future mate—the person you will marry someday.

Don't think about dating not as a game, or a casual pastime, but as a serious way to evaluate who could be the person you spend the rest of your life with. This may feel like a heavy topic right now, but I promise, taking it seriously now will save you a lot of disappointment and heartache later. Choosing a life partner is not just about attraction or fun, it's about building a relationship that will sustain you both through life's challenges and joys.

Dating With Purpose

Here's the first thing to understand: dating is a tool; it's not about the meaningless accolades you get for dating the Homecoming Queen or Star Athlete. Its purpose isn't just to go out, have fun, or collect experiences. Dating is a process through which you evaluate compatibility, develop a deep friendship, and determine if someone is the right person for a lifelong commitment.

Think of dating like a job interview, but instead of evaluating skills and experience, you're evaluating character, values, and long-term compatibility. Every date, conversation, and interaction is a small piece of information that helps you understand whether this person could be your future mate.

Practical Tip: Always date with intention. Ask yourself: "Does this person share my values, goals, and vision for the future—or are they just really cute?"

Where To Find Your Future Mate

- The great news is you can find your future mate almost anywhere! School, the gym, a sporting event, and church are just a few examples. The key is to find them where you're already involved, in places that highlight the qualities you want in a mate.
- Want someone well-educated? Go to a lecture at the museum.
- Want someone athletic? Go for a run in the park.

You'll often find people with shared values where you're already active. You find "them" where "you" are and thereby discover some basic commonality.

Caution: Picking someone up at a bar is very rarely the basis for a long-term relationship. Dating a coworker can often lead to awkward situations, especially if you break up. Avoid these scenarios, even if you spend a lot of time there.

Building a Strong Foundation

A strong relationship with a potential future mate is rooted in friendship. When dating, you're evaluating a potential mate, look beyond superficial qualities. Physical attraction is temporary, it changes over time. What lasts is character, compatibility, and shared goals. Before you ever think about romance or physical attraction, focus on developing:

- **Mutual respect:** Respect is non-negotiable. It shows up in how you communicate, resolve conflicts, and support each other's growth.

- **Shared values:** These include faith, morals, work ethic, family priorities, and life goals. Alignment on core principles is crucial.

- **Open communication:** The ability to discuss hopes, fears, finances, and life decisions honestly and respectfully.

- **Emotional support:** Both of you should feel safe to be vulnerable without fear of judgment.

- **Compatible goals:** Discuss education, career, family size, values and lifestyle choices early. Discuss your faith and your political leanings.

- **Emotional maturity:** Can this person handle conflict constructively? Can they apologize and take responsibility?

- **Financial compatibility:** Attitudes toward money, saving, and spending can make or break a long-term relationship.

- **Character and integrity:** Observe how they treat others, not just you. Integrity in small things reflects integrity in life. How do they treat the wait staff? How do they treat their family members? How do they treat their other friends and yes, even pets?

Friendship is the foundation of attraction, love, and partnership. If friendship isn't solid, the relationship is likely going to struggle under pressure.

Traits and compatibility are more important than charisma, popularity, or even shared hobbies. These are the foundation that form the backbone of a strong, lasting relationship.

Boundaries and Respect

Setting clear boundaries is essential in any dating relationship. Boundaries protect your emotional, mental, and physical well-being. They also demonstrate self-respect and help your partner understand what matters to you.

- **Emotional boundaries**: Guard your heart from being overly vulnerable too soon. Healthy relationships develop trust gradually. Establish a solid friendship first—don't "fall in love" before you know the other person; you might just be "falling in lust."

- **Physical boundaries:** Decide what you are comfortable with and communicate it clearly. Respect is shown when both partners honor these limits. Physical intimacy connects you on a different level. Discuss your feelings, values and desires. Discuss your timelines. However, if one person is "no" when it comes to the ultimate physical intimacy, that boundary must always respected without question.

- **Time and priorities:** Ensure your relationship allows room for personal growth, family, school, and work. Discuss downtime needs, family commitments, and activity preferences. Establish what is acceptable for both of you.

Boundaries aren't barriers, they create safety, respect, and clarity. They make a relationship healthier and more sustainable.

Dating Multiple People

You may date several people before finding "the one." That's okay. The goal isn't to rush into a relationship for the sake of being in one; it's to explore compatibility, learn about yourself. You'll gain clarity on what you need in a lifelong partner.

Practical Tip: Focus on one person at a time. Dating multiple people simultaneously often leads to confusion, hurt feelings, and miscommunication.

- **Avoid casual, aimless dating:** Be intentional so you don't unintentionally hurt someone. While you can learn from each relationship, don't let it become a habit of superficial dating or connections.

- **Focus on growth:** Every relationship should teach you something about yourself, communication, or what you truly value. Even if it ends, take the lessons and experiences with you.

Dating with purpose is about identifying potential, not merely entertainment. It's about cultivating meaningful relationships that could evolve into lifelong partnerships.

For the entertainment aspect, group outings are a smart way to observe potential partners from a safe distance, gauge character, and evaluate compatibility without heavy one-on-one commitment. Take it slow; this isn't a race.

Communication: The Lifeblood of a Healthy Relationship

Effective communication is the cornerstone of a successful relationship. From the first date throughout marriage, the ability to express your feelings, discuss challenges, and share hopes and dreams determines the health of the relationship.

- **Be honest:** Don't hide your values, goals, or concerns. Transparency builds trust. If what you believe is mutual and rings true with the other person, keep exploring. If it doesn't ring true, cut your time and move on quickly.

- **Listen actively:** Pay attention to what your partner is saying. Ask questions for clarity. Also remember that actions speak louder than words. Are they consistent? Listen AND observe.

- **Address conflicts early:** Don't let resentment build. Approach disagreements with patience, empathy, and a problem-solving mindset. If the conflict is something that comes up often or just one more thing on top of another, then it's time to cut bait. Don't become so invested in making it work, that you lose yourself and beliefs in the process.

Strong communication prevents misunderstandings and strengthens the bond between you and your partner. If it's right, you'll know. If it's not right, you'll know that too.

Spiritual and Moral Compatibility

Shared faith or moral alignment is often overlooked, but critical. Similar spiritual or moral perspectives guide major life decisions and create a unified framework for handling challenges.

- **Shared vision:** Discuss how you approach your faith, family, community, personal growth and beliefs. What are your deeply held convictions about life's purpose? Do they align? Do you have alignment on future aspirations, including family life, career, and how to live a fulfilling life?

- **Ethical alignment:** How do you handle honesty, responsibility, and decision-making? Do you have agreement on fundamental principles of right and wrong? Do you have shared principles like loyalty, empathy, commitment, and the pursuit of personal growth and happiness?

- **Durability**: While shared hobbies are enjoyable, shared values provide the deeper substance and resilience needed to sustain a relationship through difficulties and the inevitable changes in life.

- **Faith-based practices:** Shared beliefs will create unity and purpose in the relationship. This alignment creates a strong foundation for relationships, allowing partners to grow spiritually together, navigate life's challenges with a unified perspective, and find a deep, lasting bond through shared purpose and understanding.

When you participate in spiritual activities together, such as prayer, worship, Bible study, or community service, it fosters a deep connection and a unified foundation. A common spiritual foundation provides a source of hope and a framework for making decisions together, strengthening the relationship's resilience.

Practical Tip: Make sure you're not "unequally yoked," as the Bible warns (2 Corinthians 6:14). Shared spiritual principles build a strong foundation for lifelong partnership. It's important to consider if both partners have a similar level of passion and devotion to their faith.

Compatibility in spirituality doesn't mean perfect or identical practices, but alignment in core principles and values.

Pressure from peers, media, or society can cloud judgment. Keep your focus on what will matter decades from now. Culture often pushes young adults toward instant gratification, physical attraction, social status, and popularity. Resist the temptation to prioritize these over your spiritual beliefs and long-term compatibility.

Physical Attraction

Now don't get me wrong, we all know you're not going to date someone who physically repulses you but remember "beauty is in the eye of the beholder". Physical attraction matters, but it shouldn't be your #1 priority. Beauty fades and preferences change. Focus more on character, lifestyle compatibility, and shared values.

Consider lifestyle alignment: Are you both active, adventurous, or relaxed? Differences aren't wrong, but you must know if you can function with them long-term. You may be someone who runs 5 miles every morning. Ask yourself if you would be compatible with a couch-bound gamer? Although each of those activity choices might impact a physical fitness attribute for both people, that is something that goes beyond physical and goes more to core beliefs and lifestyle. Neither activity is right or wrong, but they do indicate how the person functions. Can you function with the broad difference in lifestyle priorities?

Be flexible even with things that don't change. You may be attracted to guys six feet tall or you may melt at her baby blue eyes, but focusing on the physical, you'll miss out on someone wonderful who is shorter or has brown eyes.

Age and Cultural Differences

Age and maturity: Consider where you are on life's path. Similar experiences and future goals make alignment easier.

Don't get up on your high horse on this, here me out. When it comes to age, I'm not talking about how old you are, sort of. I'm talking about age and maturity differences, how far each of you are down the path on life's journey.

Someone who is at approximately the same place on the path gives you commonality, similar future goals and similar life experiences. For instance, you both grew up liking the same style music, favorite bands and television shows or you both experienced the same news-worthy events from similar vantage points.

Conversely, someone 20-30 years your senior has a different set of life experiences. Their journey is farther down the path. This could be fine, but it's something to be mindful of and discuss. Their journey may have taken the beyond wanting children or already having them. You'll need to consider if you are ready for an immediate family or if you will never have children. They may not like your style of music, and you may think theirs are "the oldies".

Also consider looking way down the road, you'll need to be prepared for the potential of becoming a caretaker for an older spouse or potentially caring for their elderly parents in your home at the same time you're getting your career going or raising your own children. Again, I'm not saying it's right or wrong, just something you need to consider.

- **Cultural habits:** Environmental differences—like hobbies, vacation styles, or family traditions—may seem small now but can create tension later. Know what you can or cannot live with long-term.

When looking at cultural differences, and I'm not talking about demographics, geography or nationality, I'm talking about environmental differences. How or where you grew up is not necessarily an obstacle, but it could be.

Let's start with something simple. You may love the beach and that's where you've always gone on vacation. The other person hates the beach because they burn to a crisp and prefers touring museums. It may seem small now, but are you willing to never go on vacation to the beach again? You may very well be okay with it, but you need to ask yourself that question, so you don't resent it 10 years from now.

Does the potential mate have a cultural habit that you can't stand, like smoking or picking their nose or burping loudly at the end of a meal? It may be endearing now or just slightly icky now, but in 5 years, you'll be arguing about it being gross and getting on your nerves every time they do it!

People don't change. Those cute little idiosyncrasies now can cause you lots of grief later. People show you who they are by their actions. Believe them. Engrained behaviors and cultural habits usually don't change.

There are core learnings that may be bigger and violate your cultural views and core values. You may be a vegetarian, and your potential mate may have grown up on a cattle ranch. How will you feel going home to visit the family or even moving closer to live with them and work the ranch? Know yourself well enough to understand the cultural differences and things you can or can't live with long term.

Age difference, heritage and upbringing do not change.

Compatibility

Self-Reflection: Be the Person Your Person Wants

Before expecting traits in a partner, evaluate yourself. Go back to the FACE Chapter. Are your habits, values, and lifestyle aligned with what your ideal mate would want?

- What qualities are you bringing to the relationship?
- Do you have traits, habits, characteristics that would be off-putting to your "perfect person"?

Take a good hard look in the mirror, figuratively and literally. Are you reflecting qualities you want to give to your mate? Are you partying too much, but you want someone grounded and studious? Are you a couch potato, but you want someone athletic and outdoorsy?

Evaluate yourself so you can "Be the person, that your person will want." It may be necessary for you to do some self-assessments and make your own improvements so you can be your best self for your future mate.

You're expecting a lot, be prepared to give a lot as well. Being the best fit for your future mate requires work and commitment on your part. Get yourself ready.

Final thoughts: Remember, once you have found "the one", there is another group of people to consider before tying the knot. Once you marry, your partner's family becomes part of your life and your new extended family. In-laws can be supportive, or they can be a nightmare. Ensure you and your partner align on major family fundamentals to avoid future conflict, for if you don't align, know that your partner will usually side with the family of origin.

Reflection Questions

Here are some questions to guide your thinking about a future mate:

1. What values are non-negotiable for me in a partner?
2. What characteristics and attributes in a partner are most important to me?
3. What are my absolute "deal breakers"? What are my absolute "must haves" or "must be"?
4. How do I want to handle finances, family, and life priorities with a future spouse?
5. How do I communicate under stress, and how would my potential partner handle conflict?
6. Am I dating with intention, or am I following trends and expectations?
7. What lessons have I learned from past relationships that will inform future choices?

8. Are there changes I need to make in myself before committing to someone else?

Writing your reflections will give clarity and help you approach dating with purpose and awareness. It perfectly fine to make a list of the qualities you want in a future mate. It will help you stay focused on what's important to you.

Lifelong Perspective To Find Your Future Mate

Choosing a future mate is one of the most significant decisions you'll make. A strong, compatible partner contributes to your happiness, personal growth, and life success.

By approaching dating with intentionality, focusing on values and character, and building a foundation of friendship, you increase the likelihood of a lasting, meaningful relationship.

Remember, physical attraction fades. Shared values, mutual respect, aligned goals, and emotional maturity build marriages that endure life's challenges and thrive over decades.

Choose carefully. Take your time. Communicate openly. And never compromise on the principles that matter most to you. Be the person who your person will want. The right partner will not only complement your life but enhance it in ways you can't fully imagine yet. Your job is to do the same for your future mate.

Final Thoughts On Your Life Relationships

Think about all of your relationships intentionally. Make decisions that strengthen your character, support your growth, and help you create a meaningful, fulfilling life.

Most importantly, be the person others want to be in a relationship with. And remember ***"You are the average of the five people you spend the most time with."***~ Jim Rohn.

Favorite Points and Notes

Chapter Three

Finances

Finances

Getting Your Financial House in Order

"Financial security and independence are like a three-legged stool resting on savings, insurance and investments." ~ Brian Tracy

It's time to get your financial house in order! I know this might sound boring, or maybe even overwhelming, but skipping these steps will only make life harder down the road. The truth is simple: you should be in control of your money, not the other way around.

When most people think about money, they picture a paycheck coming in and bills going out. But there's a lot more to it than that. Building your financial house is about creating a plan, setting goals, and knowing exactly where you stand. Organization is your foundation. You can't move forward until you know where you're starting.

Step One: Gather Your Information

Pull together everything you can find about your financial life — bank statements, investment accounts, insurance policies, bills, and even your most recent tax return. You'll be using these throughout the chapter, so keep them handy, but also keep them safe and secure.

Step Two: Create Your Personal Financial Statement

Once you've got your documents in front of you, it's time to list out your **assets** (what you own) and your **liabilities** (what you owe). This simple document is called a **Personal Financial Statement**, and it tells you your **net worth**.

Don't panic if your number is small, or even negative. Everyone starts somewhere. The goal is not to feel discouraged — the goal is to measure progress. As you learn to budget, pay down debt, save, and invest, you'll watch your net worth grow over time.

Here's a simple template to get you started:

Personal Financial Statement

Assets (What You Own)

- Cash & Checking Accounts: _____
- Savings Accounts: _____
- Investments (Stocks, Bonds, Mutual Funds): _____
- Retirement Accounts (401k, IRA, etc.): _____
- Real Estate (Home, Land, Rental Property): _____
- Vehicles (Car, Boat, RV, etc.): _____
- Personal Property (Jewelry, Furniture, Electronics, etc.): _____
- Other Assets: _____

Total Assets: _____

Liabilities (What You Owe)

- Credit Cards: _____
- Student Loans: _____
- Car Loans: _____
- Mortgage(s): _____
- Personal Loans: _____
- Medical Bills: _____

- Other Liabilities: _____

Total Liabilities: _____

Net Worth = Total Assets – Total Liabilities
Net Worth: _____

(Tip: Revisit this form once a year. It's a great way to see how far you've come.)

Step Three: Build Your Financial House

Now that you know your starting point, it's time to set direction. Maybe your net worth is positive, maybe it's negative — either way, you've got a clear picture. From here, you can begin to:

- **Set Goals** — paying off debt, saving for education, buying a home, or building a retirement fund.
- **Create a Budget** — track your income and expenses so you know where your money is really going.
- **Build an Emergency Fund** — protect yourself from surprises.
- **Pay Down Debt** — free yourself from financial stress.
- **Invest for the Future** — grow your money through smart investing.
- **Protect What You Have** — with insurance, estate planning, and good habits.

Stay Organized and Monitor Progress

- **Organize Documents**: Keep deeds, wills, and insurance policies in a secure place.
- **Use a Password Manager:** Store strong, unique passwords for your financial accounts.
- **Review Regularly:** Revisit your financial plan at least once a year or after any major life change.

Getting your financial house in order isn't about being perfect — it's about taking control. With each step you complete, you're building a stronger foundation for your future. There are a lot of things to consider. We'll go over them one by one. You won't get it all done in one sitting, not even two! Take it slow and set it up right.

Ready to get started? Let's dive into your Finances!

Favorite Points and Notes

Financial Vehicles and Terms

Money management is one of the most important skills you will ever develop. The way you spend, save, and invest will shape not only your financial future but also your overall peace of mind. For young adults and anyone still learning the basics, it can be overwhelming to sort through all the different tools available. Credit cards, savings accounts, stocks, cryptocurrency—what do they all mean? Which ones are safe? Which ones are risky?

This section may feel elementary to you as it provides an overview of financial vehicles—but to know these tools and accounts inside and out will help you manage money, pay for purchases, save, and invest. For each, we'll cover its purpose, basic function, potential rewards, and risks. By the end, you'll have a clear picture of how these different options fit together in a well-rounded financial life.

Checking Accounts

Checking accounts are the foundation of modern personal finance. They are designed for everyday transactions—depositing paychecks, paying bills, writing checks, and using debit cards.

Rewards: Convenience, easy access to funds, essential for daily money management.

Risks: Typically offer no or very low interest, fees for overdrafts or minimum balance violations.

Interest-Bearing Checking Accounts

Some banks offer checking accounts that pay interest on your balance, combining the features of a regular checking account with a modest savings component.

Rewards: Earns some interest while maintaining liquidity.

Risks: Usually requires a higher minimum balance, interest rates are much lower than savings or investment accounts.

Debit Cards

A debit card looks like a credit card but works differently. It is tied directly to your checking account, and when you use it, the money is immediately withdrawn.

Rewards: Safe way to spend your own money, no risk of debt, widely accepted.

Risks: Less protection compared to credit cards in cases of fraud, no credit-building benefits, and limited rewards compared to credit cards.

Debit cards are excellent for those who want to avoid overspending and prefer to only spend money they already have.

Venmo, Zelle, PayPal, and Other Payment Apps

Peer-to-peer payment apps have transformed the way people transfer money. These services allow you to send and receive money instantly using a smartphone.

Rewards: Speed, convenience, no need for cash, widely used for splitting bills or paying friends.

Risks: Limited buyer protection compared to credit cards, potential for scams, may encourage casual overspending since transactions feel less tangible.

Money Market Investment Accounts (MMIAs)

Money Market Investment Accounts are interest-bearing accounts offered by banks or credit unions. They usually require a higher balance but provide better returns than a savings account.

Rewards: Higher interest than savings, FDIC-insured up to limits, relatively safe.

Risks: Limited withdrawals, higher minimums, interest rates still lower than long-term investments.

Savings Accounts

Savings accounts are designed for storing money safely while earning interest. They're best used for emergency funds and short-term goals.

Rewards: Safe, FDIC-insured, earns interest, highly liquid.

Risks: Low interest rates (may not keep up with inflation), limited monthly withdrawals by regulation.

Certificates of Deposit (CDs)

CDs allow you to deposit a sum of money for a fixed period (3 months, 6 months, 1 year, 5 years, etc.) in exchange for a guaranteed interest rate.

Rewards: Higher interest than savings accounts, predictable returns, FDIC-insured.

Risks: Money is locked in until maturity (penalties for early withdrawal), interest rates may lag behind inflation or better opportunities.

Treasury Bills (T-Bills)

T-Bills are short-term government securities sold at a discount and redeemed at full value when they mature.

Rewards: Backed by the U.S. government, virtually risk-free, liquid.

Risks: Lower returns than other investments, inflation may outpace gains.

Bonds

Bonds are loans you give to governments or corporations in exchange for regular interest payments and the return of principal at maturity.

Rewards: Steady income, less volatile than stocks, wide range of options.

Risks: Interest rate risk (bond values fall when rates rise), credit risk (issuer may default), inflation risk.

Mutual Funds

Mutual funds pool money from many investors to buy a diversified portfolio of stocks, bonds, or other securities. Managed by professionals, they provide an easy way for individuals to diversify.

Rewards: Diversification, professional management, accessible to beginners.

Risks: Management fees, potential underperformance, market risk.

Exchange-Traded Funds (ETFs) and Closed-End Funds (CEFs)

ETFs are like mutual funds but trade on stock exchanges like individual stocks. CEFs are similar but have a fixed number of shares and may trade at a discount or premium to their net asset value.

Rewards: Diversification, often lower fees than mutual funds, tax efficiency, flexibility to trade like stocks.

Risks: Market volatility, CEF premiums/discounts can be unpredictable.

Index Funds

Index funds are a type of mutual fund or ETF that aim to replicate the performance of a specific market index (like the S&P 500).

Rewards: Low fees, broad diversification, long-term growth potential.

Risks: Tied to overall market performance, no chance of outperforming the market.

Stocks

Buying a stock means buying a piece of ownership in a company. Stocks are one of the most powerful ways to build wealth over the long term but come with significant risk.

Rewards: Potential for high returns, dividends, ownership in growing companies.

Risks: Market volatility, company-specific risks, potential for total loss of investment.

Real Estate Investment Trusts (REITs)

REITs allow you to invest in real estate portfolios (such as shopping centers, office buildings, or apartments) without directly buying property.

Rewards: Diversification into real estate, steady dividend income, liquidity compared to physical real estate.

Risks: Sensitive to interest rates, property market cycles, management risks.

Precious Metals (Gold, Silver, etc.)

Precious metals are alternative investments often seen as a hedge against inflation and economic uncertainty.

Rewards: Tangible assets, can hold value during market downturns, diversification.

Risks: No income (unlike stocks/bonds), price volatility, storage and insurance costs.

Annuities

Annuities are insurance products that provide a guaranteed income stream in exchange for an upfront investment.

Rewards: Predictable income, can last for life, useful for long-term stability.

Risks: High fees, limited liquidity, complex terms, inflation may erode fixed payments.

Cryptocurrency

Cryptocurrencies are digital currencies like Bitcoin or Ethereum that operate on decentralized networks using blockchain technology.

Rewards: Potential for very high returns, decentralized and independent of governments, innovative technology.

Risks: Extreme volatility, regulatory uncertainty, vulnerability to hacking or scams, not widely accepted as payment.

LOANS AND LINES OF CREDIT AND THEIR PURPOSES:

1. Unsecured Loans (Personal Loans)

Definition: Loans that do not require collateral. Approval is based mainly on your creditworthiness.
Use: Debt consolidation, medical expenses, weddings, or home improvements.

- **Reward:** No collateral; flexible uses; fast approval.
- **Risk:** Higher interest rates; harder to qualify with poor credit.

2. Student Loans

Definition: Loans designed to pay for higher education costs such as tuition, housing, and fees.
Use: Provides access to education without paying full costs upfront.

- **Reward:** Federal loans may offer low rates, deferment, and income-driven repayment. Education can boost lifetime earnings.
- **Risk:** Can become a heavy debt burden; private loans often lack flexible repayment options.

3. Secured Loans

Definition: Loans backed by collateral (e.g., house, car). Lender can seize asset if borrower defaults.
Use: Common for mortgages, car loans, or business loans.

- **Reward:** Lower rates; higher borrowing amounts possible.
- **Risk:** Loss of collateral if payments are missed.

4. Car Loans (Auto Loans)

Definition: A secured loan for purchasing a vehicle, with the car itself as collateral.
Use: Allows you to buy a car without paying full price upfront.

- **Reward:** Makes vehicles accessible; generally lower interest rates.
- **Risk:** Depreciation may leave you "upside down"; repossession if you default.

5. Balloon Loans

Definition: A loan with smaller payments early on and one large lump-sum "balloon" payment at the end.
Use: Common in real estate or business financing where borrowers expect to refinance, sell, or have cash later.

- **Reward:** Lower payments in the short term; can allow access to higher-value assets.
- **Risk:** Large final payment; risk of default if you can't refinance or sell; sensitive to market downturns.

6. Mortgage Loans

Definition: Long-term loans used to purchase real estate, secured by the property.
Use: Enables homeownership and real estate investing.

- **Reward:** Builds ownership and equity; lower rates than unsecured loans.
- **Risk:** Foreclosure if payments missed; long-term debt obligation.

Note: Many types exist—**fixed-rate, adjustable-rate (ARM), FHA/VA/USDA loans, jumbo loans**—each suited to different borrower needs.

7. Equity Loans

Definition: Loans taken against the equity in your home.
Use: Major expenses like renovations, debt consolidation, or medical bills.

- **Reward:** Lower rates; can borrow large sums if equity is high.
- **Risk:** Risk of foreclosure; reduces available equity.

8. HELOCs (Home Equity Lines of Credit)

Definition: A revolving line of credit secured by home equity, similar to a credit card.
Use: Ongoing projects, renovations, or variable expenses.

- **Reward:** Flexible borrowing; lower rates than credit cards.
- **Risk:** Variable rates; overspending risk; foreclosure if unpaid.

9. Lines of Credit

Definition: Flexible loans allowing borrowing, repayment, and re-borrowing up to a set limit. Can be secured or unsecured.
Use: Cash flow gaps, emergencies, business expenses.

- **Reward:** Interest only on amount borrowed; quick access.
- **Risk:** Easy to misuse; variable rates may increase costs.

10. Credit Cards

Definition: A type of revolving credit that lets you borrow up to a limit and repay later. Provides convenience, fraud protection, rewards, and helps build credit if used responsibly.
Use: Everyday purchases, emergencies, rewards programs.

- **Reward:** Convenience, rewards programs (cash back, travel points), credit-building.
- **Risk:** Very high interest rates; debt traps if carrying a balance; potential negative credit impact.

Example: A $10,000 balance at 22% with only minimum payments could take 30+ years to repay, with over $25,000 in interest!

11. Peer-to-Peer (P2P) or Hard Money Loans

Definition: Non-traditional loans from individuals or private lenders. Hard money loans are often short-term, asset-backed (common in real estate deals).
Use: Quick funding for personal or real estate needs.

- **Reward:** Fast access; flexible approval criteria.
- **Risk:** Very high interest; strict repayment; loss of collateral in defaults.

Loan Types by Repayment Structure

Term Loans

Definition: Borrow a lump sum, repay in fixed installments over a set term.
Use: Common for mortgages, auto loans, and business loans.

- **Reward:** Predictable payments; straightforward.
- **Risk:** Less flexibility; obligation persists until fully paid.

Revolving Credit

Definition: A credit line that allows repeated borrowing and repayment up to a set limit.
Use: Ongoing purchases, cash flow flexibility.

- **Reward:** Flexible; only pay interest on balance.
- **Risk:** Easy to accumulate high-interest debt.

Interest-Only Loans

Definition: Borrower pays only interest for an initial period; later payments include principal.
Use: Often in real estate or specialized business loans.

- **Reward:** Lower initial payments; short-term flexibility.
- **Risk:** Payments jump later; may owe a large balance still.

Other Loan Considerations

Fixed vs. Variable Rates

Fixed: Same rate throughout loan → stability and predictable budgeting.
Variable: Rate tied to market → lower at times, but monthly payments can rise.

Other Terms To Know

1. DRIPs (Dividend Reinvestment Plans)

Definition: A DRIP automatically reinvests the dividends you earn from stocks or funds back into purchasing more shares instead of paying you in cash.
Use: Helps you grow investments through compounding without having to manually reinvest.

- **Reward:** Accelerates growth since you're buying more shares automatically (compounding effect). Often no commission fees.
- **Risk:** If the stock price falls, you're still buying more of it. Less flexibility because you're not receiving cash you could use elsewhere.

2. Liquid Assets

Definition: Assets that can quickly be converted into cash without losing significant value. Examples: checking/savings accounts, stocks, bonds.
Use: Provides flexibility and security to cover emergencies, bills, or sudden opportunities.

- **Reward:** Easy access to cash; critical for emergencies and liquidity needs.
- **Risk:** Often lower returns compared to less liquid investments (e.g., real estate). Inflation can erode value if held too long in cash.

3. Fixed Assets

Definition: Long-term tangible assets used in business or personal ownership that are not easily converted into cash. Examples: property, equipment, vehicles.
Use: Provides utility, production capacity, or long-term value (e.g., rental property).

- **Reward:** Can appreciate in value (like real estate) and may generate ongoing income.
- **Risk:** Harder to sell quickly; may depreciate (like cars or machinery); higher maintenance costs.

4. Equity

Definition: The ownership interest in an asset after subtracting liabilities. For a home: equity = property value − mortgage balance. For stocks: equity = shares of ownership in a company.
Use: Shows true ownership value; grows as you pay off debt or as asset value increases.

- **Reward:** Builds net worth and can be leveraged (e.g., borrowing against home equity).
- **Risk:** Market value may decline, reducing equity. Over-leveraging (borrowing too much) can wipe it out.

5. Net Worth

Definition: The value of everything you own (assets) minus what you owe (liabilities). Formula: **Net Worth = Assets − Liabilities**.

Use: Measures overall financial health; helps track progress toward goals.

- **Reward:** Growing net worth shows increasing financial stability and freedom.
- **Risk:** Negative net worth (debts > assets) limits opportunities and can create financial stress.

6. ROI (Return on Investment)

Definition: A measure of profitability that shows how much you earn relative to what you invest. Formula: **ROI = (Gain − Cost) ÷ Cost × 100%**.
Use: Evaluates whether an investment is worthwhile compared to alternatives.

- **Reward:** Helps you identify high-performing investments and make better financial decisions.
- **Risk:** ROI can be misleading if you don't consider time, fees, or risk factors. High ROI opportunities may also carry high risk.

7. Net

Definition: The amount left after expenses, deductions, or taxes are subtracted. For example, "net income" is what you actually take home after withholdings.
Use: Shows the true, spendable or "what you keep" in finances or business.

- **Reward:** Net figures reflect reality, not inflated numbers.
- **Risk:** People sometimes confuse net with gross and overspend based on pre-deduction income.

8. Gross

Definition: The total amount before any expenses, taxes, or deductions are subtracted. For example, "gross income" is

your salary before withholdings.
Use: Useful for understanding total potential revenue or income.

- **Reward:** Gives a full picture of earnings or revenue potential.
- **Risk:** Misleading if you forget about deductions; overestimating what you can actually spend.

9. Personal Financial Statement

Definition: A document that outlines an individual's assets, liabilities, income, and expenses—basically a snapshot of financial health.
Use: Used by individuals to track finances or by lenders to assess creditworthiness.

- **Reward:** Provides clarity and control; helps you see where you stand and make better decisions.
- **Risk:** If inaccurate or incomplete, it can misrepresent your financial picture and lead to poor planning or loan denial.

Final Thoughts

Financial vehicles are tools, and like any tools, their value depends on how you use them. Some are meant for safety and stability (savings accounts, CDs, Treasury Bills), others for long-term growth (stocks, mutual funds, ETFs), and others are speculative and risky (cryptocurrency, precious metals). Credit cards or various types of loans, when used responsibly, can provide convenience and rewards, but when abused, they can become a crushing financial burden.

The most important lesson is to understand the purpose of each financial vehicle and use it appropriately. Building wealth and financial security is not about chasing the latest trend—it's about balancing risk and reward, diversifying your choices, and staying disciplined. With knowledge and wise decisions, you can create a financial foundation that supports your goals, both today and decades from now.

Favorite Points and Notes

Budgeting

Taking Control of Your Money

Budgeting. Just the word itself feels boring, doesn't it? Nobody wakes up excited to sit down with a calculator and spreadsheet. But here's the truth: budgeting is the foundation of financial freedom. Without a plan for your money, your money has a funny way of disappearing. You've probably experienced that feeling of "Where did it all go?" at the end of the month. That happens when your dollars don't have a plan.

Think of budgeting as telling your money what to do instead of wondering what it did. It's not about restriction—it's about freedom. Freedom from debt, freedom from anxiety, and freedom to make choices that matter to you. The earlier you learn how to budget, the stronger your financial future will be.

Let's walk step by step through the essentials of a budget, break down percentages that actually work, and see how you can take control of your finances—starting today.

Step 1: Fixed Expenses – No More Than 40% of Your Income

The first thing to account for is your **fixed expenses**—the bills you're required to pay every month, no matter what.

Examples include:

- Housing (rent or mortgage)
- Car loans or leases
- Student loan payments

- Insurance premiums

Here's a good rule of thumb: **fixed expenses should never be more than 40% of your monthly income**. Why? Because if you let these obligations grow too large, you'll have nothing left for savings, debt payoff, or even enjoying life.

Of that 40%, housing should take up **no more than 25%** of your income. This aligns with the calculations mortgage lenders use when deciding whether someone can actually afford a house.

If you're spending more than 25% on rent or a mortgage, it's time to rethink your housing situation. It might not be glamorous, but living in a modest apartment, having a roommate, or delaying the dream of your "perfect place" early on can give you financial breathing room.

Real-Life Example

If you make **$4,000 per month**, no more than **$1,600** should go to fixed expenses. That means:

- **Housing (25%)**: $1,000 or less
- **Other fixed bills (15%)**: $600 or less

If your rent is $1,500 and your car payment is $500, you're already at $2,000—50% of your income—before even eating or saving. That imbalance will strangle your budget.

Key Tip

When you're tempted to "stretch" your housing budget because "it's only $200 more," remember: **housing is the biggest anchor to your budget.** Keeping it modest creates freedom everywhere else.

Step 2: Retirement – 15–20% of Your Income

This might feel far away, but retirement needs to be on your radar now—not later. Believe me, you'll thank me later! Every year you wait makes it harder to catch up because you're losing out on the power of compounding.

Even small contributions made early can snowball into huge sums later. We'll go into more detail in the Retirement section.

- $200 invested monthly at age 25 could grow into over **$1 million by age 65**, assuming a 10% annual return.
- Waiting until age 35 to start means you'd need to save more than **double** to catch up. That 10 years makes a huge difference.

Where to Put It

- **Employer Retirement Plan (401k, 403b, TSP)**: Contribute at least enough to get the match if offered. It's free money.
- **Roth IRA**: Great for young adults since withdrawals in retirement are tax-free.
- **Traditional IRA**: Another option if your income or tax situation makes it better.

Key Tip

Think of retirement contributions as a bill you must pay every month—**pay yourself first**. If you only save what's left over, you'll never save enough.

Step 3: Regular Savings – 10% of Your Income

Retirement is long-term, but you also need savings for the here and now. **10% of your income should go into savings**, broken down into three categories:

1. **Immediate Emergency Fund**
    - Build at least **$1,000** quickly. This is not for shoes, vacations, or concert tickets. It's for real emergencies: car repairs, a broken hot water heater, or an unexpected medical bill.
2. **Long-Term Emergency Fund**
    - After the $1,000 is in place, work toward saving **3–6 months of living expenses**. This protects you in case of job loss or illness that keeps you from working.
3. **Targeted Savings**
    - Save separately for specific goals—Christmas, vacations, a wedding, or a down payment on a house. Keep these funds in a different account so they don't get mixed into your everyday spending.

Key Tip

Use **separate savings accounts** or digital "buckets." Many banks now let you label accounts: "Emergency Fund," "Vacation," "Car Replacement." This visual separation prevents you from accidentally dipping into your long-term fund for short-term fun.

Step 4: Variable Expenses – 15–20% of Your Income

Variable expenses are the costs that change each month. They're essential, but also the area where you have the most control.

Examples include:

- Utilities (electricity, water, internet, phone)
- Groceries (not just food, include household items like cleaning supplies too)
- Transportation (gas, maintenance, insurance if not fixed)
- Clothing (this means dry cleaning existing clothes too)
- Entertainment and eating out
- Streaming services and subscriptions
- Personal care (haircuts, toiletries, etc.)
- Pet expenses (food, vet bills, grooming)

Plan **15–20% of your income** for this area. It's also the first place to look if your budget isn't balancing.

Real-Life Example

If you're spending $700 a month eating out and then wondering why you can't save, the math is right here. A budget isn't magic—it's simply telling the truth about your habits.

Key Tip

This is where **cash envelopes or digital envelope apps** shine. If entertainment is your weak spot, give yourself $200 in cash or in a designated app wallet. When it's gone, it's gone.

Step 5: Charitable Giving – 10% of Your Income

Generosity should always be part of your budget. Why? Because giving does two things:

1. It helps others.
2. It reminds you that money is a tool, not a master.

Designating **10% of your income to giving**—whether that's to your church, a nonprofit, or someone in need—keeps you grounded and grateful.

Debt: The Weight That Holds You Back

If you're carrying debt—credit cards, student loans, personal loans, car payments—your budget will feel tighter than it should. That's why paying off debt is a priority.

How to get rid of it:

1. List debts from smallest to largest.
2. Pay minimums on all except the smallest.
3. Throw every extra dollar at the smallest until it's gone.
4. Once the smallest is paid off, take the payment you were making on that one and add it to the next smallest debt.
5. Repeat until they're all gone.

Why the smallest first? Because behavior beats math. You need quick wins to stay motivated. Some people start with the highest interest rate first, but that doesn't necessarily get you the momentum you need, especially if it takes you years to pay it off. When you're done paying off the smallest, you can add that $50 payment to the next smallest bill where you were making $100 minimum payment and now get more bang for the buck with a $150 payment! Make sense?

Putting It All Together: Example Budget

Let's look at how this plays out with a **$4,000 monthly income**:

- **Fixed Expenses (40%)**: $1,600
    - Housing (25%): $1,000
    - Other fixed bills (15%): $600
- **Retirement (15%)**: $600
- **Savings (10%)**: $400
- **Variable Expenses (20%)**: $800
- **Charitable Giving (10%)**: $400
- **Debt Payoff (Extra Funds)**: Any leftover should attack debt.

Notice how each dollar you earn is accounted for? That's intentional and your "extra money" won't disappear like it was never there.

Practical Tips for Successful Budgeting

- **Budget as a Team**: If you're married, do this together. Unity matters.
- **Talk About Spending Habits**: Recognize whether you're a saver or spender.
- **Give Yourself Grace**: You'll mess up in the beginning. That's okay. Just keep adjusting and stay focused.
- **Don't Rely on Credit Cards**: They're a crutch that leads to debt.
- **Prioritize Essentials**: Always cover food, housing, utilities, and transportation first.
- **Overestimate Expenses**: Especially in the beginning—better to have extra than come up short. If you've got extra, put it on a debt!
- **Review Past Spending**: Use your last 4–6 months of statements as a mirror.
- **Cut Unnecessary Expenses**: Cancel subscriptions, cook at home, buy secondhand.
- **Adjust Monthly**: Your budget should reflect your real life, not an idealized version.
- **Use Cash for Problem Areas**: Especially food, entertainment, or shopping.

- **Add a Miscellaneous Line**: Something will always come up.
- **Assign Leftover Money**: Savings or debt payoff—don't let it vanish.

Mindset Matters

Budgeting isn't about saying "no." It's about saying "yes" to what matters most.

- A budget lets you take that trip guilt-free—because you saved for it.
- A budget helps you buy a car in cash—because you planned it.
- A budget frees you from credit card anxiety—because you're in control.

The real key is consistency. The longer you practice, the easier it becomes.

Final Thoughts

Budgeting isn't glamorous. It won't make headlines on social media. But it will give you something better: peace of mind, confidence, and options.

When you give every dollar a job, you don't wonder where your money went—you tell it where to go. And that's the difference between drifting through life broke and building a future you're proud of.

Budgeting isn't about saying "no."
It's about saying "yes" to the things that matter most—without stress, guilt, or debt.

Favorite Points and Notes

Income

From One Paycheck to Seven Streams of Income

Why and What are seven streams?

You and I both know what it feels like to depend on a single paycheck. It's exciting when that first direct deposit hits, then it becomes routine, and before long it's your one lifeline. But here's the hard truth: one income stream is a fragile way to live. Jobs change. Markets shift. Life happens. Millionaires understand this, which is why they typically cultivate at least **seven distinct streams of income**. The point is to be resilient. If one stream weakens, the others keep you steady.

In this section, I'll show you how to start with the paycheck you already have, then layer additional streams—profit from a small business or side hustle, interest and dividends from investments, cash flow from rentals, growth from capital gains, and royalties from intellectual property—until you've built a diversified, durable income system. I'll also give you a roadmap for the next decade so you can see how to go from one stream to seven without burning yourself out. Remember this isn't a sprint, it's a very very long marathon.

Take a deep breath. You don't need to master everything today. You just need to start, learn, and keep moving.

1) Earned Income — the foundation you stand on

Let's start with the one you already know: your job. Whether you're scanning badges at the gym, stocking shelves, coding computer programs, or guiding customers through a sale, **earned income** is the first stream for nearly everyone. It keeps the lights on, it builds your résumé, and it funds your next moves.

What it is

Money exchanged for your time and skills—wages, salary, tips, overtime, bonuses and commissions.

Why you should keep that J.O.B.

Earned income is your launch pad. It's how you finance your emergency fund, your first investments, the laptop for your side hustle, or the down payment that moves you into real estate. Entry jobs in many U.S. markets may pay **$40,000–$55,000**; specialized early-career roles might land **$60,000–$75,000** after a couple of promotions. Annual raises can hover around ~3% in many companies, with bigger jumps when you switch roles or employers.

How to maximize it now

- **Skill-up intentionally.** Target skills with market pull: sales, data, coding, UX, project management, compliance, trade certifications.
- **Negotiate early.** A one-time $3,000 raise echoes into future raises and compounding savings.
- **Earn credibility.** Volunteer for visible, measurable projects. Be the person who delivers.
- **Track your real hourly rate.** Include commute, unpaid overtime, and stress. This helps you decide

which side hustles or certifications are worth it when you add them to your plate.

Pitfalls

- **Time ceiling.** You can't scale your hours forever.
- **Burnout.** Guard your energy. Building more streams requires you at your best.

Your goal: use your paycheck to make tomorrow's additional income streams possible.

2) Profit Income — small business, side hustles, and selling value

Have you ever made something people wanted and paid you for? That's **profit income**—the money left after your business brings in revenue and pays expenses. It can be as simple as tutoring algebra on Saturdays or as involved as launching a boutique e-commerce brand.

Why this stream matters

Profit income breaks the "paid only for time" ceiling. It can be scrappy and small at first, then grow to something substantial. It also teaches you priceless skills: pricing, marketing, operations, customer service, and systems.

Example: I'll first take myself as an example. I have multiple streams of income, some are side hustles that enhance or correlate to my main career, others are passions that not only bring in additional funds, but they also fill my heart. For you, it may be that you work in a marketing department creating graphics on a computer all day. In the evening, you may consider doing marketing or social media management for a small local business. On the other hand, you may need a break from sitting at a computer and you may want your evening to be for exercise and movement. If that's the case, why not incorporate a dog walking business into your evening exercise or teach Pilates? The point is, you know yourself best. Analyze what you enjoy and figure out how to make money doing it!

Popular side hustles and small businesses

- A freelance content creator charging **$300/article** for 4 articles a month adds **$1,200/month** before expenses.
- A local dog-walking route with 10 clients at **$20/walk**, 3 days a week, can hit **$2,400+/month**.
- A micro-agency that bundles social media, light design, and scheduling for five local businesses at **$450/month** each earns **$2,250/month** gross.
- **Freelance services:** writing, editing, Virtual Assistant, bookkeeping, social media management, web/UX design, baking, tutoring.
- **Tutoring & coaching:** academic subjects, test prep, fitness, music, language, career prep.
- **Digital products:** templates, ebooks, stock photos/video, light SaaS plug-ins.
- **E-commerce:** print-on-demand, niche drop shipping, handmade or curated goods.
- **Local services:** pet care, lawn care, house cleaning, moving help, event photography.
- **Content monetization:** affiliate sites, newsletters, YouTube, podcasts

How to start without driving yourself crazy

1. **Validate demand first.** Ask five prospective customers, "Would you pay $X for Y?"
2. **Start lean.** Free/cheap tools, low overhead, minimal inventory.
3. **Deliver like a pro.** Clear scope, on-time delivery, responsive updates.
4. **Build a simple system.** Templates, checklists, invoicing routine, weekly marketing habit.
5. **Reinvest profits.** Upgrade tools, build a site, run small ads, outsource low-value tasks.

Pitfalls

- **Overextending your schedule.** Keep your day job strong. This is your primary source of income. Don't blow it!
- **Neglecting taxes and structure.** Track income and expenses, consider an LLC, talk to a tax pro.
- **Inconsistent demand.** Keep marketing weekly, even when busy. Automate it.

Your goal: prove you can make profit on your own terms—then steadily refine and scale.

3) Interest Income — letting your cash earn while you sleep

Picture your savings working a quiet night shift. **Interest income** is what you earn by letting banks or borrowers use your money. It's steady, often lower risk, and forms part of your safety net. This is the "you need money to make money" category.

What it is

Interest from high-yield savings, Certificates of Deposit (CDs), U.S. Treasuries and other fixed-income instruments.

Examples

- High-yield savings accounts currently around ~4% APY.
- CDs potentially ~4–5% depending on term.
- Conservative bond funds or laddered Treasuries offering yields that can be attractive relative to recent years.

How to use it

- **Emergency fund FIRST.** Target 3–6 months of expenses in high-yield savings. Leave it and let it grow.
- **CD ladder.** Stagger maturities so part of your cash earns more while some stays liquid.
- **Reinvest interest.** Compounding is subtle early, powerful later.

Pitfalls

- **Inflation.** Real returns can be lower than they look.
- **Liquidity traps.** Don't lock away money you'll need soon.

Your goal: stabilize your base with interest income so you can take smart risks elsewhere.

4) Dividend Income — "thank-you" checks for being an owner

Imagine owning a tiny slice of a company you respect, and it pays you a little share of profits just for holding. That's **dividend income**—quiet, compounding, and surprisingly motivating.

What it is

Cash distributions from companies or funds, usually quarterly. You can automatically reinvest them through DRIPs (Dividend Reinvestment Plans). Reinvest for growth, or take the check if you want to expand another of your businesses.

Examples

- A diversified dividend ETF yielding ~**2.5–4%**.
- Owning 100 shares in a company that pays **$2.50/share** annually = **$250/year** before taxes.
- A $50,000 dividend portfolio at **3.5%** yields **$1,750/year**, which you can reinvest.

How to build it

- **Start broad.** Consider a quality dividend ETF or index fund.
- **Reinvest automatically.** Let DRIPs buy more shares for you.
- **Diversify sectors.** Don't chase a single high-yield sector.
- **Evaluate sustainability.** Focus on firms with strong free cash flow and a history of payout growth.

Pitfalls

- **Yield traps.** Sky-high yields can mask trouble.
- **Cuts happen.** Companies can reduce or suspend dividends.
- **Taxes.** Understand qualified vs. ordinary dividends.

Your goal: accumulate dependable ownership income and let compounding quietly work.

5) Rental Income — monthly cash flow from real assets

If you like tangible investments, **rental income** turns property into monthly cash flow. It can start small—renting a spare room—and grow into a portfolio that pays you while it appreciates.

What it is

Income from leasing space: spare room, basement apartment, duplex, single-family home, small multi-family, or even storage units or parking.

Examples

- A two-bedroom condo purchased at **$250,000** might rent for **$1,800–$2,200/month** in some markets. After mortgage, HOA, taxes, insurance, maintenance, and vacancy, **net** yields in many areas can land around ~4–6% annually.
- A house-hack (you live in one unit and rent the other) can reduce your housing cost dramatically.

Getting started

- **House hack.** Live in one side of a duplex or add a basement suite.
- **Try a room first.** Short-term or mid-term rental of a spare room builds experience.
- **Run real numbers.** Track mortgage, taxes, insurance, maintenance, vacancy, management.
- **Team up early.** Build your team with a good real-estate agent, lender, and property manager. They are worth gold.

Pitfalls

- **Over-leverage.** Don't stretch so thin that one vacancy breaks you.
- **Underestimating costs.** Set aside real reserves for repairs and turnovers. I always figure an 80% occupancy rate making sure I can handle 20% vacancy and still make a profit.
- **Regulatory surprises.** Know your local rules, especially for short-term rentals like AirBNBs. Not all localities allow them.

Your goal: build a cash-flowing asset base that also has a shot at appreciating over time.

Note: If you buy $250,000 worth of stock, how much will it cost you? That's not a trick question, it will cost $250,000. But if you buy a $250,000 house, it will cost you $50,000 (your 20% down payment) plus expenses. If you rent that house for the amount of your mortgage payment plus a few hundred dollars, you're making a profit at the same time someone else is paying you the funds needed to pay the mortgage. At the same time, you're gaining equity in the house through appreciated value. (Remember my 80% occupancy rate when you figure profit.) This is why so many millionaires have Real Estate in their portfolio. (Not to mention the tax advantages.)

6) Capital Gains — buying right, holding smart, exit well

You've probably heard stories of someone buying an asset and selling years later for a life-changing profit. **Capital gains** are the difference between what you paid and what you sell for. They're not a paycheck; they're the big step-ups.

What it is

Profits realized when you sell stocks, real estate, a business, collectibles, or crypto for more than your cost basis.

Examples

- Buy a stock at **$20**, sell at **$40** years later → **$20 gain/share** (minus taxes).
- Buy a starter home at **$200,000**, improve and sell for **$350,000** years later → gain less costs/taxes.

How to think about it

- **Long-term mindset.** Favor patient, high-quality holdings over random swings.
- **Trim carefully.** Take partial profits to rebalance, not just all-or-nothing.
- **Re-deploy gains.** Move proceeds into new opportunities or safer baselines.

Pitfalls

- **Market timing.** Even the experts can't time the market exactly. It's tempting—and costly—to try to guess tops and bottoms. Watch the trends or hire a professional.
- **Tax drag.** Short-term gains often face higher rates; know your thresholds.
- **Concentration risk.** A big win can anchor your emotions. Keep diversifying.

Your goal: Invest in assets that increase in value so when it's sold you've realized a profit.

7) Royalty & Licensing — get paid for ideas, over and over

What do you know so well you could package it and sell it? A skill, a method, a story, a song, a system. **Royalty and licensing income** pay you repeatedly for work you created once.

What it is

Ebooks, courses, music, software licenses, stock photos/videos, paid templates, patents—assets others pay you to use.

Examples

- A short ebook at **$15** that sells **200 copies/year** = **$3,000/year** less fees.
- A course at **$200** with **300 enrollments/year** = **$60,000/year** gross (after marketing and platform fees).
- A lightweight software plug-in at **$10/month** with **500 subscribers** = **$5,000/month** gross.

How to build it

- **Validate first.** Pre-sell to a small audience or run a survey to determine popularity.
- **Polish the product.** Design, clarity, and outcomes matter.
- **Pick channels.** Amazon KDP, Udemy, Gumroad, your own site, or a licensing deal.
- **Market consistently.** A weekly newsletter, short-form video, or partner promos.
- **Protect the IP Intellectual Property.** Clear licensing terms, basic legal protections like copyrights or trademarks.

Pitfalls

- **Platform risk.** Rules change; make sure you own your email/customer list.
- **One-hit mentality.** Build a small catalog of similar ideas you can expand.
- **Silence after launch.** Plan marketing and distribution, it's just as important as creation.

Your goal: create once, earn repeatedly, and expand a small catalog over time.

Putting it together: your decade roadmap (from 1 to 7)

It's natural to think, "This is a lot." You're right. It is. So let's pace it. You'll layer streams gradually, using each one to fund the next. Here's a sample **10-year progression** you can adapt.

Phase 1 (Years 1–2): Foundation & breathing room

- **Streams:** Earned Income + Interest
- **Moves:** Get or stabilize your job. Build a 3–6 month emergency fund in a high-yield account (Leave it alone, no borrowing for cute shoes or vacations).
- **Wins:** A buffer against surprise bills; less stress; time to think clearly.

Phase 2 (Years 2–3): Experiment wisely

- **Streams:** Add Profit (side hustle), begin Dividends (small).
- **Moves:** Launch one side hustle with the highest chance of quick validation. Start automated contributions to a broad dividend ETF; turn on DRIP.
- **Wins:** Proof that you can make money outside your job; the first trickle of owner income.

Phase 3 (Years 3–5): Systematize & ship an asset

- **Streams:** Earned + Profit + Interest + Dividends + (first Royalty/License).
- **Moves:** Turn your best skill into a small digital product (ebook, course, template). Create lightweight systems for your side business.
- **Wins:** Your first "create once, earn many times" check. More confident cash management.

Phase 4 (Years 5–7): Step into real estate

- **Streams:** Add Rental; continue building the others.
- **Moves:** Consider house hacking or a small duplex. Track numbers conservatively. Assemble your team (agent, lender, inspector, manager).
- **Wins:** Monthly rental cash flow + equity growth; a new kind of diversification.

Phase 5 (Years 7–10): Optimize, rebalance, and scale

- **Streams:** All seven in motion (to varying degrees).
- **Moves:** Prune low-ROI (Return on Investment) hustles, double down where margins are healthiest. Reinvest in rentals or royalty catalog. Rebalance your portfolio annually.
- **Wins:** Less reliance on earned income; greater freedom to choose how you spend your time.

Remember: this is a model, not a mandate. Your path might emphasize royalties over rentals, or vice versa. The point is intentional pacing.

Managing risk without losing momentum

- **Keep buffers.** Maintain your cash reserves for life and for each property or business.
- **Avoid over-leverage.** Debt can magnify gains—and stress. Choose wisely.
- **Diversify, but don't scatter.** Build two or three strong streams before you add more.
- **Protect your health.** Don't get overwhelmed! Sleep, exercise, and set boundaries that are not optional.

- **Use pros.** A tax professional can save you major mistakes. Their fees are well worth keeping you on target as your streams multiply.

A quick guide to taxes and structure (talk to a pro)

- **Track everything.** Keep clean records for income and expenses by stream.
- **Choose simple entities first.** Many start as sole proprietors, then form an LLC as revenue grows.
- **Understand deductions.** Home office, mileage, software, education may apply.
- **Plan for quarterly taxes.** Side businesses often require estimated payments.
- **Separate accounts.** Give each business its own bank account. Clarity is power.

Mindset shifts that change everything

- **From consumer to creator.** Each week, ask: what did I create that can earn for me later?
- **From hours to assets.** Look for one-to-many systems (content, code, templates, rentals).
- **From random to rhythmic.** Weekly marketing, monthly reviews, annual rebalancing.
- **From fear to experiments.** Keep stakes small, feedback fast, and learning constant.
- **Time Block:** Don't let it consume you. Schedule your tasks on your calendar and stick to it, but don't overwhelm yourself or you won't stick to it!

Putting your first week into motion

If we were sitting together with coffee, here's what I'd ask you to do over the next 7 days:

1. **Map your money.** What's your net monthly surplus after essentials?
2. **Pick one side hustle to test.** Determine customer interest level. What resources or training do you need?
3. **Open/optimize your high-yield savings.** Start your savings and/or your emergency fund.
4. **Start or automate investing.** Even $50/week builds the habit and momentum.
5. **Brainstorm a first digital asset.** What is one problem you can solve for someone else in 10–20 pages or a short video series.
6. **Calendar a weekly review.** Same time, every week. Track progress, adjust, repeat.

You won't get to seven streams in a month. But in a month, you can be unmistakably on your way.

Summary: Income

Depending on one paycheck makes your finances very fragile. One layoff or illness can ruin you financially. Millionaires typically build **seven income streams** for resilience, freedom, and choice. You don't need all seven today—start with one, layer steadily, and reinvest wisely. Congratulations! You're on your way to financial freedom!

Favorite Points and Notes

Insurance

When you first start thinking about insurance, it can feel like stepping into a maze, full of confusing terms, endless options, and what seems like unnecessary paperwork. You might wonder why you even need it, or whether it's just a way for companies to take your money. The truth is, insurance isn't about saving money or investing for your future, it's about protecting yourself from financial risks that could completely wipe you out if something unexpected happens.

Imagine this: you're in college or just starting your career, and you're playing in a weekend soccer league or participating in a long-distance hike. You twist your ankle badly or maybe break your leg. Suddenly, you're facing surgery, rehabilitation, and, if you're employed, weeks off work. The medical bills alone could easily reach $40,000 to $50,000. Without insurance, you would have to pay these costs out of pocket, potentially setting yourself back years financially.

Before we go any further, here's a key principle to remember: insurance exists to transfer financial risk that you cannot manage on your own. It is a shield against events that could be financially catastrophic, not a savings or investment tool. You do not need coverage for minor, manageable expenses, like routine checkups or minor dental procedures. Insurance is about covering the things that could truly derail your life financially if they happen unexpectedly.

With that in mind, let's walk through the types of insurance you should consider, and break them down so you can make informed decisions about your future. I'll also include tips and examples that are especially relevant for young adults navigating their first jobs, apartments, or big purchases.

1. Health Insurance

Health insurance is non-negotiable. You need it, and here's why. Think of it as protection for the unexpected. Health insurance isn't about covering every minor inconvenience, it's about shielding you from medical expenses that could be financially devastating.

Imagine this scenario: you and your partner welcome your first child. Even with a standard, uncomplicated birth, hospital fees, doctor visits, and postnatal care can cost $15,000 to $20,000. Health insurance ensures you don't have to pay these massive bills out of pocket, letting you focus on recovery and caring for your new baby instead of worrying about financial ruin. Without health insurance, you'd be responsible for paying for that yourself, which could take years to recover from financially.

Health insurance isn't meant for minor ailments, like hangnails or colds. Those are costs you can manage yourself. It is about preparing for events that could financially overwhelm you.

Here are some tips to make health insurance more affordable:

- **Employer-sponsored plans:** If your job offers coverage, this is often the most cost-effective option. Employers usually pay part of your premium, which can save you hundreds of dollars each month.
- **High-deductible plans with Health Savings Accounts (HSAs):** If you're generally healthy and can handle higher costs in an emergency, a high-

deductible plan will lower your monthly premiums. HSAs allow you to save pre-tax dollars for medical expenses, which is a huge advantage.

- **Health share programs:** These are not technically insurance but can be a more affordable option. Members share costs for medical expenses, which can make it easier for young adults with lower budgets to afford coverage.

Practical tip: always check the network of doctors included in your plan, the coverage for specialists, and prescription drug costs. Being proactive now can save you headaches and unexpected bills later.

2. Long-Term Disability Insurance

Even if you are young and healthy, you need to plan for the possibility of long-term disability. Short-term illnesses or injuries can usually be handled with an emergency fund covering three to six months of expenses, but what if something keeps you from working for months or even years?

Long-term disability insurance replaces a portion of your income if you cannot work due to illness or injury. Around 1 in 4 young adults will experience a disabling condition before reaching retirement age. Typically, this insurance covers 60–70% of your income. The cost is generally 1–3% of your annual salary, depending on the risk level associated with your occupation.

Here's an example: you work a desk job, so your risk is relatively low, and your premiums are modest. Compare that to a friend working construction, where the job is physically demanding, and the cost of premiums is higher. Either way, long-term disability insurance ensures your bills are covered, giving you peace of mind that an accident or illness won't derail your financial stability.

3. Long-Term Care Insurance

Long-term care insurance may feel like something for the distant future, but it's worth considering now. By the time you reach your sixties or seventies, you might need help with daily activities, whether through in-home care, assisted living, or a nursing home.

The costs are staggering in 2025: private nursing home rooms start at $10,000 to $15,000 per month. Assisted living facilities often cost thousands monthly, and in-home care can also add up quickly. Medicare generally does not cover these costs, meaning waiting too long to buy coverage could wipe out your retirement savings.

Purchasing long-term care insurance at a younger age generally results in lower premiums. A good policy covers assisted living, in-home care, and nursing home stays. Never bundle this insurance with life insurance, as additional features can increase the cost unnecessarily. Even if you don't set this up now, put it on your "to do" list for the future and don't wait until retirement age to start.

4. Life Insurance

Life insurance replaces your income if you die. If anyone depends on you financially, whether a partner, children, or other family members, it's essential.

There are several types of life insurance, and each serves a different purpose:

- **Term Life Insurance:** Provides coverage for a specific period, typically 10–20 years. This is straightforward and affordable, ideal for covering immediate responsibilities like a mortgage, student loans, or childcare costs.

- **Whole Life Insurance:** Offers lifelong coverage with a savings component, accumulating cash value over time. Premiums are higher, but it provides lifelong security.

- **Indexed Universal Life Insurance (IUL):** Flexible policies where growth of cash value is linked to a market index. Offers both a death benefit and the potential for value accumulation.

The best policy depends on your current needs and long-term goals. Many young adults start with term insurance and explore other types, like Whole Life or IUL, later as their finances and family responsibilities grow.

5. Renters Insurance

If you are renting, your landlord's insurance only covers the building, not your belongings. Renters insurance protects your personal property, covers liability if someone is injured in your apartment, and reimburses additional living expenses if your unit becomes uninhabitable.

For most young adults, $20,000–$50,000 in coverage is usually sufficient. Policies are typically inexpensive, sometimes $15–$25 per month. Think of it as a small investment to protect your possessions and your peace of mind.

Practical tip: take an inventory of your belongings and document their value. This makes filing claims easier if something goes wrong. Make note of any property or items that are particularly expensive or collectables.

6. Homeowners Insurance

When you buy a home, homeowners insurance is a must. It protects your house, belongings, and liability. Mortgage Companies will require that you carry Homeowners Insurance in an amount at least enough to cover the dwelling because the house stands as the collateral for their loan and the insurance thereby covers their investment. Important coverage includes:

- **Extended dwelling coverage:** Pays to rebuild your home.

- **Personal property:** Covers your belongings.

- **Liability:** Protects you from injuries or damages occurring on your property.

- **Additional living expenses:** Covers temporary housing if your home is uninhabitable.

Flood and earthquake coverage are usually separate, so check whether you need a rider or separate policy. Always review your policy annually to ensure coverage keeps pace with changes in property value or new purchases.

7. Title Insurance

Title insurance protects you when purchasing a home. It ensures that the property title is free of disputes, liens, or claims. Essentially, it gives you confidence that the house you are buying is legally yours. Without it, you could face significant legal issues if a previous owner's claim arises later. Again, the Mortgage Company will require Title Insurance to protect their investment, but an Enhanced or Extended Title Insurance policy will further protect you. This is typically a one-time purchase that you pay for at the settlement or purchase of the property.

8. Deed Theft Protection

Deed theft occurs when someone fraudulently transfers your property title to another party. Deed theft protection monitors your property records and provides assistance if fraudulent activity is detected. This is especially useful for young adults purchasing their first home, offering an extra layer of security against potential fraud. Check during your home purchase and your Title Policy, sometimes Deed Theft protection is included as part of that policy.

9. Identity Theft Protection

Identity theft is becoming increasingly common as more of your financial life moves online. Even if you aren't responsible for fraudulent charges, resolving identity theft can be a lengthy and stressful process, including repairing credit and dealing with banks or legal authorities.

A good identity theft protection policy provides monitoring, restoration services, and guidance to repair the damage efficiently. Some policies also alert you to suspicious activity, helping you act quickly to prevent financial loss.

10. Umbrella Policy

An umbrella policy provides extra liability protection beyond your auto and homeowners policies. If your net worth is $500,000 or more, an umbrella policy is highly recommended. It protects against lawsuits or claims that exceed your current coverage limits. Premiums are usually $200–$300 per year for $1 million in coverage, which is a small price for major peace of mind.

For example, imagine a scenario where you cause a minor car accident, but the other driver exaggerates injuries and sues for damages that exceed your standard auto insurance coverage. An umbrella policy covers the excess, keeping your personal assets safe.

Final Thoughts

When you look at insurance this way, it no longer feels like a pile of confusing forms or boring paperwork, it's a way to build a safety net, protecting you, your loved ones, and your finances from unexpected events. By understanding what each type of insurance does, you can make informed decisions that keep your future secure without paying for unnecessary extras.

Insurance is a tool for taking control of your life, protecting what matters most, and ensuring that one unexpected event does not derail years of hard work. Start with the essentials, consider additional coverage based on your situation, and review your policies regularly as your needs change.

By taking these steps, you are not just buying insurance, you are building a strong foundation for your future. That is one of the smartest things you can do as a young adult.

Quick Reference Chart

Insurance Type	Purpose / What It Covers	Recommended Coverage / Notes	Estimated 2025 Costs
Health Insurance	Protects against catastrophic medical expenses	Choose plan that covers major medical events, includes preferred doctors and hospitals, consider High Deductible + HSA if healthy	$250–$600/month (individual, employer-sponsored), $500–$1,200/month (family)
Long-Term Disability	Replaces portion of income if unable to work	Covers 60–70% of your salary, choose coverage based on occupation risk	1–3% of annual salary
Long-Term Care Insurance	Covers assisted living, in-home care, or nursing home care	Policy should include in-home care, assisted living, and nursing home	$200–$400/month (varies by age at purchase and coverage amount)
Term Life Insurance	Replaces income if you die during coverage term	10–12x annual income for financial dependents	$25–$50/month for $500,000 policy (healthy 25–30-year-old)

Insurance Type	Purpose / What It Covers	Recommended Coverage / Notes	Estimated 2025 Costs
Whole Life Insurance	Lifelong coverage + cash value accumulation	Permanent coverage, builds savings over time	$200–$400/month for $500,000 policy (young adult)
Indexed Universal Life (IUL)	Flexible death benefit + market-indexed cash value growth	Lifelong coverage, flexible premiums, optional growth tied to market index	$150–$350/month depending on coverage and age
Annuities	Guarantees income during retirement	Choose fixed or variable, ensures you don't outlive savings	$100–$500/month or lump sum depending on plan
Auto Insurance	Covers accidents, damages, liability	Minimum liability: $500,000 (split 250/500/250), add collision, comprehensive, PIP/Med Pay if available, uninsured/underinsured motorist	$100–$250/month for full coverage (varies by age, car, location)

Insurance Type	Purpose / What It Covers	Recommended Coverage / Notes	Estimated 2025 Costs
Renters Insurance	Protects personal property, liability, additional living expenses	$20,000–$50,000 coverage, includes liability and additional living expenses	$15–$25/month
Homeowners Insurance	Protects home, personal property, liability	Coverage for dwelling, property, liability, additional living expenses, add flood/earthquake riders if needed	$100–$300/month depending on home value and location
Title Insurance	Protects against property title disputes	One-time purchase during home closing	$1,000–$3,000 depending on home price
Deed Theft Protection	Protects against fraudulent transfer of property title	Monitors property records, recovery assistance if fraud occurs	$20–$50/month
Identity Theft Protection	Protects personal identity and credit	Policy should include monitoring, restoration, and support	$15–$30/month

Insurance Type	Purpose / What It Covers	Recommended Coverage / Notes	Estimated 2025 Costs
Umbrella Policy	Additional liability coverage beyond auto/home	Recommended if net worth ≥ $500,000, covers lawsuits exceeding regular policy limits	$200–$300/year for $1 million coverage

Favorite Points and Notes

Investment Strategies

Building Wealth with Wisdom

Why Strategy Matters

When it comes to investing, the difference between success and failure is rarely luck. It is almost always strategy. You can earn, save, and budget faithfully, but if you do not invest wisely, your money will not work for you. Investing is about letting your dollars grow without you having to trade your time for them. Think of every dollar as a little employee — each one should be out there earning more dollars while you focus on school, work, family, or your personal goals.

The purpose of this section is to help you understand not just *what* to invest in, but *how* to think about investing. A good strategy helps you stay steady through ups and downs, avoid costly mistakes, and maximize your long-term growth.

The Foundation — Mindset and Goals

Before we even talk about stocks, bonds, or real estate, we need to discuss mindset. Investing is not about getting rich quick. It is about building wealth slowly and securely over time. Ask yourself:

- What is my time horizon? (Are you investing for retirement 40 years from now, or for a down payment in 5 years?)

- What is my risk tolerance? (How much could you lose in a downturn before you panic and sell?)
- What are my financial priorities? (Do you want stability, growth, income, or a mix?)

Your answers will shape the right investment strategies for you. If you are 21 and starting fresh, you can afford to take on more risk for long-term growth. If you are 40 with kids, you might lean more toward stability. Strategy always starts with self-awareness.

Core Principles of Investing

These are truths you need to remember every step of the way:

1. **Start Early**: Time is your most powerful ally. Compounding makes small amounts grow into large amounts when given decades.
2. **Stay Consistent**: Investing regularly matters more than timing the market.
3. **Diversify**: Never put all your eggs in one basket. Spread across asset classes and industries.
4. **Keep Costs Low**: Fees, commissions, and fund expenses eat away at returns.
5. **Avoid Emotion**: Fear and greed cause most investment mistakes. Stick to your plan.

Risk and Reward

Every investment has two sides — risk and reward. Stocks can deliver 10% average returns over decades, but in the short term, you might lose 30% in a single year. Bonds are steadier, but usually yield less. Real estate can build wealth, but it can also tie up cash and demand maintenance. Bank Savings Accounts and Certificates of Deposit are FDIC insured so they are very low risk, but your potential reward is more modest. Commodities like physical gold or silver can be rewarding, but liquidity is very limited.

A good strategy balances risk and reward. Think of it like building a plate of food: you want a variety of nutrients, not just one. Your portfolio should have growth investments, stability investments, and income investments.

The Power of Compounding

Compounding is the engine of wealth. If you invest $500 a month starting at age 21, earning 10% annually, by age 65 you would have around $4.1 million. If you wait until age 40 to start with the same $500 a month, you would only have about $617,000. The difference is not just what you put in — it is the time compounding had to work for you.

The earlier you start, the less you have to sacrifice later. That is why you should never wait until you "feel ready." Start with whatever you can afford, even if it is just $50 a month. Build it into your Budget and pay yourself first!

Active vs Passive Investing

There are two main schools of thought:

- **Active Investing**: Trying to pick winning stocks, time the market, or choose "hot" sectors. This takes time, skill, and luck. Most professionals fail to beat the market consistently.
- **Passive Investing**: Buying index funds or ETFs that track the whole market. This method is low-cost, requires little effort, and historically outperforms most active managers.

For most young adults, passive investing is the smarter choice. You do not need to outguess Wall Street — you just need to ride along with the market's long-term growth.

Asset Classes and Their Roles

1. Stocks (Equities)

- Represent ownership in a company.
- High growth potential but volatile.
- Best for long-term goals like retirement.
- Strategies: Buy broad index funds (S&P 500, Total Market) or sector ETFs (technology, healthcare).

2. Bonds (Fixed Income)

- You loan money to governments or corporations. They pay you interest.
- Safer than stocks but with lower returns.
- Provide stability and income in a portfolio.

3. Real Estate

- Tangible, can generate rental income and appreciation.
- Can hedge against inflation.
- Requires management and often debt (mortgage).
- REITs (Real Estate Investment Trusts) are a hands-off alternative.

4. Cash and Cash Equivalents

- Savings accounts, CDs, money market funds.
- Safe but earn little.
- Useful for emergency funds, not long-term growth.

5. Alternative Investments

- Gold, commodities, private equity, cryptocurrency.
- High risk and unpredictable.
- Should only be a small slice of your portfolio, if at all.

Building a Portfolio

A portfolio is your collection of investments. How you divide money between stocks, bonds, and other assets is called *asset allocation*.

- Young adults might go 80% stocks, 15% bonds, 5% cash.
- Middle-aged investors might shift to 60% stocks, 30% bonds, 10% cash.
- Near retirement, 40% stocks, 50% bonds, 10% cash may feel safer.

Diversification within each asset class also matters. Do not just buy one stock or one bond fund. Spread across many companies, sectors, and even countries.

Strategies for Long-Term Success

Dollar-Cost Averaging

Invest a fixed amount on a regular schedule, no matter what the market is doing. This reduces the risk of bad timing and builds discipline.

Buy and Hold

Own investments for years or decades. Avoid chasing trends or trying to jump in and out. Time *in* the market beats timing the market.

Rebalancing

Periodically adjust your portfolio back to your target allocation. For example, if stocks grow too much and you become too risky, sell some and move into bonds.

Dividend Investing

Choose companies or funds that pay regular dividends. These can provide steady income and reinvested growth.

Growth vs Value

- Growth investing targets companies expanding rapidly.
- Value investing targets companies undervalued relative to fundamentals.
  Many investors combine both approaches.

Common Mistakes to Avoid

- **Panic Selling** during downturns.
- **Over-concentration** in one stock or sector.
- **High Fees** from expensive mutual funds or trading too often.
- **Speculation** in "get rich quick" schemes like penny stocks.
- **Ignoring Taxes** — capital gains and dividends can reduce returns if not managed wisely.

Special Topics for Young Adults

Investing in Retirement Accounts

- **401(k)**: Employer-sponsored, often with matching contributions (free money).
- **IRA/Roth IRA**: Individual accounts with tax advantages.
- Always prioritize accounts with tax benefits before investing in taxable accounts.

Emergency Fund Comes First

Never invest money in long term investments that you might need in the short term. Build a 3-6 month emergency fund before aggressive investing.

Balancing Debt and Investing

If you carry high-interest debt (like credit cards at 20% APR), paying it off is a better "investment" than chasing stock returns.

Advanced Strategies (for later)

Once you are experienced and financially stable, you may explore:

- Options trading (risky, not recommended for beginners).
- Leveraged real estate.
- Angel investing or startups.
- International diversification.
- There are many more advanced strategies but stick to the basics to start. You'll learn these with experience.

Do not jump ahead until you have mastered the basics.

Staying the Course

Markets will go up and down. News headlines will scare you. Friends will brag about quick profits. None of that should shake your plan. The most successful investors are not the ones who chase fads — they are the ones who stay consistent, patient, and disciplined.

Final Thoughts

You do not need to be a financial genius to succeed. You just need to understand the principles, avoid major mistakes, and stay committed for the long haul. Investing is not about beating others; it is about building the life you want.

Bullet-Point Synopsis

- Strategy matters more than luck.
- Start with mindset: goals, risk tolerance, and time horizon.
- Follow core principles: start early, stay consistent, diversify, keep costs low, avoid emotion.
- Compounding is the ultimate wealth builder.
- Passive investing (index funds, ETFs) often outperforms active strategies.
- Understand asset classes: stocks, bonds, real estate, cash, alternatives.
- Build a balanced portfolio and rebalance over time.
- Use proven strategies: dollar-cost averaging, buy and hold, dividend investing.
- Avoid common mistakes: panic selling, over-concentration, high fees, speculation, ignoring taxes.
- Focus first on retirement accounts, emergency funds, and paying down high-interest debt.
- Advanced strategies can come later, but basics must come first.
- Long-term success requires patience and discipline.

At-a-Glance Summary

Core Principles

- **Start Early**: Compounding is most powerful when given decades.
- **Stay Consistent**: Invest regularly; time in the market beats timing the market.
- **Diversify**: Spread across stocks, bonds, real estate, and more.
- **Keep Costs Low**: Choose low-fee funds and avoid frequent trading.
- **Control Emotion**: Stick to your plan, not market headlines.

Risk & Reward

- **Stocks**: High growth, high volatility. Best for long-term.
- **Bonds**: Lower return, more stability and income.
- **Real Estate**: Tangible, income-producing, but ties up capital.
- **Cash/Equivalents**: Safe but low growth; best for emergencies.
- **Alternatives**: Gold, crypto, etc. — risky, should be small allocation.

Portfolio Basics

- Young adult: ~80% stocks, 15% bonds, 5% cash.
- Middle age: ~60% stocks, 30% bonds, 10% cash.
- Near retirement: ~40% stocks, 50% bonds, 10% cash.
- Rebalance periodically to maintain risk balance.

Proven Strategies

- **Dollar-Cost Averaging**: Invest fixed amounts on schedule.
- **Buy & Hold**: Long-term ownership of broad funds or stocks.
- **Dividend Investing**: Reinvest or collect steady cash flow.
- **Growth + Value Mix**: Blend of high-growth and undervalued companies.

Priorities for Young Adults

1. Build an **emergency fund** (3–6 months of expenses).
2. Pay off **high-interest debt** before aggressive investing.
3. Maximize **retirement accounts** (401(k), IRA, Roth IRA).
4. Expand into taxable accounts once basics are covered.

Common Mistakes to Avoid

- Panic selling in downturns.
- Over-concentration in one stock or sector.
- Paying high fees or chasing trends.
- Ignoring taxes and long-term planning.

Quick Takeaway

Investing is not about gambling or quick wins. It's about strategy, patience, and discipline. Start early, stay consistent, diversify, and let compounding do the heavy lifting.

Favorite Points and Notes

Retirement Plans

Understanding the Accounts That Shape Your Future

When you think about retirement, it may feel like something far off in the distance—something you'll deal with later. But here's the truth: your future self will either thank you or resent you based on the choices you make today. The sooner you understand retirement plans, the better positioned you'll be to live life on your terms decades from now.

The first thing you need to know is that a **retirement plan is simply the type of account** you use to save and grow your money for the future. The **plan is not the investment itself**. Within each plan, you'll have different investment options—like mutual funds, index funds, ETFs, or even company stock. Think of the plan as the basket, and the investments as the fruit you put inside it. Choosing the right basket matters, but so does choosing the right fruit.

Let's break this down step by step so you can see the difference between the various plans available, the investment choices within them, and how you can use them to build long-term wealth.

Employer-Sponsored Retirement Plans

Employer-sponsored plans are accounts you get access to through your job. These often come with tax advantages and sometimes even **free money** in the form of employer matching contributions. If you work for a company that offers one, this is usually the easiest way to start saving for retirement.

401(k) Plans

The most common employer retirement account, a 401(k) allows you to contribute a portion of your salary before taxes. The money grows tax-deferred until you withdraw it in retirement, at which point you'll pay ordinary income taxes.

- **Roth 401(k)**: Some employers also offer a Roth option. Contributions are made with after-tax money, but withdrawals in retirement are tax-free.
- **Employer Matching**: Many companies will match part of what you contribute—for example, 50% of the first 6% of your salary. That's free money. If your employer offers a match, always contribute enough to get the maximum benefit.

403(b) Plans

Similar to a 401(k), but for employees of public schools, churches, and certain nonprofits. Contribution limits and tax treatment are nearly identical.

457 Plans

Typically offered to government employees and some nonprofits. Contributions are pre-tax, and withdrawals are taxed as income. One unique benefit: 457 plans don't always have early withdrawal penalties if you leave your job before age 59½.

SIMPLE IRA Plans

Designed for small businesses with 100 or fewer employees. Employers must either match employee contributions (up to 3%) or make a 2% non-elective contribution for each eligible employee. These are simple and affordable for small companies to offer.

SEP IRA Plans

Simplified Employee Pension plans are primarily for self-employed people or small business owners. Contributions come only from the employer (which may be you if you're self-employed).

Defined Benefit Plans (Pensions)

These are traditional pensions, where your employer promises to pay you a set amount every month in retirement based on your salary and years of service. They're less common today, but if you work in certain industries or for government agencies, you may still have one.

Cash Balance Plans

A hybrid between a pension and a 401(k). Your employer credits your account each year with a percentage of your salary plus interest. The account balance then grows predictably over time.

Employee Stock Ownership Plans (ESOPs)

Some employers let you build ownership in the company through stock allocation. This ties your retirement savings to company performance, which can be a benefit—or a risk if the company struggles.

Individual Retirement Arrangements (IRAs)

If your employer doesn't offer a retirement plan—or even if they do—you can open your own IRA. This gives you more flexibility and control over your investment choices.

Traditional IRA

You contribute pre-tax money (depending on income and eligibility), your investments grow tax-deferred, and you pay taxes when you withdraw in retirement.

Roth IRA

You contribute after-tax money, but withdrawals are completely tax-free in retirement if certain conditions are met. For young adults, Roth IRAs are often the best long-term bet because your tax rate now is likely lower than it will be later.

Other Options

- **Solo 401(k)**: For self-employed individuals with no employees. Contribution limits are higher than IRAs, allowing you to save more.
- **Taxable Accounts**: Regular brokerage accounts without tax advantages. More flexible but less tax-efficient.
- **Health Savings Accounts (HSAs)**: If paired with a high-deductible health plan, HSAs can serve as a stealth retirement account because contributions are tax-deductible, growth is tax-free, and withdrawals for medical expenses are tax-free.
- **Non-Qualified Deferred Compensation Plans**: Often offered to executives, these allow you to defer income into the future with fewer restrictions, but also fewer protections.

Defined Benefit vs. Defined Contribution

When people talk about retirement plans, they usually fall into two categories:

1. **Defined Benefit Plans**: These promise a set payout in retirement. The employer manages the investments and takes the risk. Examples: pensions and cash balance plans.
2. **Defined Contribution Plans**: These promise a set contribution each year, but your retirement benefit depends on how well the investments perform. You take the risk. Examples: 401(k), 403(b), and IRAs.

Employer-Directed vs. Self-Directed Plans

This is where the distinction between the **plan** and the **investment options** becomes crystal clear.

- **Employer-Directed Plans**: In a typical 401(k), your employer chooses the investment menu. You may have a dozen mutual funds to pick from, but you can't invest in just anything you want. The advantage is simplicity, but the downside is limited choices.
- **Self-Directed Plans**: With an IRA or Solo 401(k), you get to decide where to invest. Your options are much broader: stocks, bonds, index funds, ETFs, even real estate in some cases. The flexibility is greater, but so is the responsibility to choose wisely.

The key is understanding that the **plan is the container**. What goes inside—the investments—is what determines your growth potential.

Automatic Investing: The "Forced" Way to Save

One of the biggest advantages of retirement plans is that they make investing automatic.

- **Employer Payroll Deductions**: With 401(k)s and similar plans, your contributions are taken out of your paycheck before you even see the money. This makes saving effortless.
- **Employer Matching**: Think of this as an instant return on investment. If your employer matches 50% of your contributions up to 6% of your salary, you're effectively earning a 50% guaranteed return on that portion.
- **Automatic Transfers for Self-Funded Accounts**: If you have an IRA or brokerage account, you can set up recurring monthly transfers. This creates a habit of saving without having to think about it.

Automatic investing works because it removes human emotion. You don't forget, you don't second-guess, and you don't skip. It just happens. Over decades, that consistency builds real wealth.

The Penalties of Waiting to Start

One of the biggest mistakes young adults make is putting off retirement saving. You may think, "I'll start later when I'm making more money," but every year you wait costs you dramatically. Why? Because of the power of compound growth.

Let's look at two examples.

- **Starting at Age 21**: You invest $500 per month until age 65. At an average 10% annual return, your account grows to about **$4.1 million**.

- **Starting at Age 40**: You invest the same $500 per month until age 65. At the same 10% return, your account grows to only about **$617,000**.

The difference is staggering—more than **$3.4 million**. That's the penalty for waiting. The earlier you start, the less money you have to contribute out of your own pocket to end up with far more later. Time is your most valuable asset when it comes to retirement planning, and it's the one thing you can never get back.

Choosing the Right Retirement Plan

So, how do you decide which plan is best for you? It depends on your situation:

- If your employer offers a **401(k) with matching funds**, contribute at least enough to get the full match. Don't leave free money on the table.
- If you're eligible, open a **Roth IRA**. It's one of the best long-term vehicles for young adults.
- If you're self-employed, consider a **Solo 401(k)** or **SEP IRA** to maximize contributions.
- If you already max out other options, you can add taxable accounts or HSAs to your strategy.

The reality is you don't have to pick just one. Many people use a combination—like contributing to a 401(k) at work while also funding a Roth IRA on the side.

The Bottom Line

Retirement planning is not just for people nearing the end of their careers—it's for you, right now. The earlier you start, the more powerful compound growth becomes.

Remember: the **plan is the account type**, and the **investments are what you put inside the plan**. Employer-directed plans give you convenience and matching funds but limited options. Self-directed plans give you flexibility and control but require more decision-making.

Whatever route you take, commit to automatic saving, take advantage of employer matches, and diversify your investments. Retirement may feel far away, but the steps you take today will shape the freedom and security you enjoy later.

And as always—this is not financial advice. Your situation is unique, and tax and retirement laws change. Consult a financial advisor or tax professional before making major decisions.

Start early, stay consistent, and let compound interest do the heavy lifting.

At-a-Glance Summary: Retirement Plans

- **Plans vs Investments**: Plans are account types; investments are what you put your account into.
- **Employer-Sponsored Plans**: 401(k), 403(b), 457, SIMPLE IRA, SEP IRA, pensions, ESOPs.
- **Individual Plans**: Traditional IRA, Roth IRA, Solo 401(k), HSAs, taxable accounts.
- **Defined Benefit vs Defined Contribution**: Pensions promise a payout; 401(k)/IRA depend on investments.
- **Employer-Directed vs Self-Directed**: Limited options vs wide flexibility.
- **Employer Match**: Always contribute enough to capture free matching funds.
- **Automatic Investing**: Payroll deductions and transfers make saving effortless.
- **The Penalty of Waiting**: Start at 21 ($4.1M) vs start at 40 ($617K)—a $3.4M difference.
- **Best Approach**: Use multiple accounts when possible; diversify and start early.

Favorite Points and Notes

Last Will and Testament and Other Essential Documents

I know—it's not the most exciting topic. Thinking about death, estate planning, or what will happen to your stuff when you're gone isn't exactly a fun Saturday afternoon activity. But here's the reality: unless you're immortal, someone is going to get your belongings someday. The only question is, who decides—and how messy it will be for your loved ones. That's where a Last Will and Testament, or simply a will, comes in.

A will is a legal document that lays out your instructions for how your property and assets should be distributed after your death. It also allows you to designate guardians for minor children or dependents and appoint someone you trust to manage your estate. Without a will, state laws determine how your property is divided, which can lead to unnecessary stress, conflicts among family members, and delays in distributing your assets.

Here's what every young adult should know about creating a will—and why it's more important than you might think.

Why Having a Will Matters

Many people assume that wills are only for the wealthy. That's a myth. Regardless of the size of your estate, a will ensures your wishes are honored and protects the people you care about most. Here's why having a will is so important:

1. **Clear Distribution of Assets**
   A will spells out who gets what and when. Whether

it's money, a car, heirlooms, or even a collection of vinyl records, a will eliminates uncertainty and prevents disputes among family members.

2. **Protect Your Loved Ones**
   Without a will, your assets might go to relatives you wouldn't have chosen. A clear will ensures your estate benefits the people you care about, not distant cousins you barely know.
3. **Appoint a Guardian for Minor Children**
   If you have kids under 18, you can name a guardian in your will. Otherwise, the courts decide who takes care of them, which may not align with your wishes. Even if you're married, it's important for both parents to have separate wills to ensure guardianship plans are legally sound.
4. **Faster Access to Assets**
   A will simplifies the probate process, allowing your heirs to access their inheritance more quickly and reducing stress during an already difficult time.
5. **Tax Planning and Charitable Giving**
   Wills allow you to plan for taxes and include charitable donations if you wish. While estate taxes affect only large estates, other tax considerations may still apply, and a well-drafted will helps your estate handle these efficiently.

What a Will Covers—and What It Doesn't

A will allows you to specify how your property, bank accounts, personal items, and other assets should be distributed. It can also include instructions for charitable contributions or the care of pets. However, there are some things a will doesn't control:

- **Life Insurance Proceeds**: These go directly to designated beneficiaries.
- **Transfer-on-Death (TOD) or Payable-on-Death (POD) Accounts**: Investment and bank accounts

with named beneficiaries bypass the will. If a beneficiary passes away before you, the asset usually reverts to your estate.
- **Spousal Rights**: Some states have elective-share laws that entitle a spouse to a portion of your estate, even if your will specifies otherwise.

A will also allows you to appoint an executor, the person responsible for administering your estate. Executors ensure bills are paid, assets are distributed according to your wishes, and any legal matters are handled appropriately. This role can be assigned to a family member, trusted friend, or attorney.

Understanding Probate

Probate is the court-supervised process of validating your will and distributing your assets. When someone dies, their estate usually goes through probate unless everything is already arranged to transfer outside of it. Probate involves filing paperwork with the court, notifying heirs and creditors, settling debts, and finally distributing assets.

Why does probate matter? Because it can be **slow, expensive, and public**. Attorneys' fees and court costs can consume a portion of your estate, and the process can take months—or even years. Even modest estates can get stuck in probate delays. This is why so many estate planning strategies focus on minimizing or avoiding probate altogether.

If you take no action, probate is unavoidable. But with some planning, you can make the process much easier on your family. Naming beneficiaries on accounts, setting up trusts, and creating transfer-on-death deeds are all ways to reduce the time and cost of probate.

Types of Wills

Not all wills are created equal. Here are the main types you should know about:

1. **Simple or Testamentary Will**
   The most common type, a simple will allows you to clearly outline your wishes. It's signed in front of witnesses, usually two adults who are not beneficiaries, making it legally enforceable.
2. **Holographic Will**
   Handwritten by you without witnesses, these are only recognized in some states and are more likely to be challenged.
3. **Mirror Wills**
   Typically used by married couples, mirror wills allow each spouse to direct property to the other or to children, with the surviving spouse retaining flexibility to update their own will.
4. **Joint and Mutual Wills**
   Joint wills are signed by two people in a single document, and mutual wills are agreements that bind one spouse to the terms of the other after death. Both are less flexible than mirror wills and generally not recommended.
5. **Pour-Over Will**
   Used in conjunction with a trust, this type ensures that any assets not already placed in the trust are transferred there upon death.

Trusts: Another Key Piece of the Puzzle

While wills are essential, they are not the whole picture. Trusts are powerful tools that give you more control over your assets and often help you avoid probate.

Revocable Trust

Also called a living trust, this type of trust allows you to remain in control of your assets during your lifetime. You can add, remove, or change beneficiaries, and you can revoke the trust entirely if you change your mind. The main advantage is that when you pass away, assets in the trust transfer directly to your beneficiaries without going through probate.

Irrevocable Trust

Unlike a revocable trust, once you establish an irrevocable trust, you generally cannot change it. Why would anyone do that? Because irrevocable trusts offer strong protection from creditors, potential lawsuits, and estate taxes. If you want to shield assets for your children or grandchildren, this type of trust can be valuable.

Why a Trust Matters Even for Young Adults

You may not think of yourself as wealthy, but if you own a home, have life insurance, or even just want to ensure that what you do own transfers smoothly, a trust can save your loved ones money, time, and stress. Trusts are not only for millionaires—they are for anyone who values peace of mind.

Essential Documents

Taking steps today to shield your wealth for your children—whether that's your home, $1,000, or millions—means creating a set of documents that work together. Here are the essentials:

1. **A Trust**
   As already mentioned, a trust is a necessity. It keeps you in control and allows your heirs to inherit without the complications of probate.

2. **A Will**
   Even with a trust, you need a will. The will "pours over" your remaining possessions into the trust and names guardians for minor children.
3. **Financial Power of Attorney**
   This document appoints someone to manage your finances if you are unable to. It can be temporary or permanent, and it ensures your bills, taxes, and accounts are handled without interruption.
4. **Advance Medical Directive**
   An advance directive outlines your medical wishes if you cannot speak for yourself. It can specify your views on life support, resuscitation, organ donation, and more.
5. **Durable Power of Attorney for Health Care**
   This document names someone you trust to make healthcare decisions on your behalf. It is often combined with or included in the advance directive.
6. **Living Will**
   A living will is a written statement of your healthcare preferences, similar to an advance directive. It ensures doctors and family members know what you want.
7. **Do Not Resuscitate Order (DNR)**
   A DNR tells medical staff not to perform CPR if your heart stops. It is an intensely personal decision, but one worth considering and documenting.
8. **Transfer-On-Death Deed (TOD)**
   If you own a home, filing a TOD deed with your county allows your heirs to inherit the property without going through probate. This can save them thousands of dollars and months of frustration.
9. **Funeral Planning Declaration**
   This allows you to specify your wishes for burial, cremation, or services. Without it, your family may face stress and disagreements during a very emotional time.

Practical Steps to Get Your Affairs in Order

- Put beneficiaries on all your financial accounts: checking, savings, CDs, life insurance, retirement plans, and investments. Beneficiaries override wills, so keep them updated.
- Create a written list of all accounts, passwords, credit cards, utilities, loans, and insurance policies. Keep it in a safe place.
- Make sure someone you trust has access to your safe deposit box or knows where your important documents are stored.
- Keep titles for all vehicles, boats, and campers in a place where heirs can find them.
- Discuss your plans with your heirs and with those you've appointed to act for you. Explaining your choices now avoids misunderstandings later.
- Review your documents regularly. Life changes quickly, and your paperwork should reflect your current reality.

Costs of Estate Planning

Creating some of these documents can be free with online resources, while others require legal guidance. A basic will might cost $300–$1,000 through an attorney. A trust may cost more, but it can save your family many times that amount in probate expenses. Think of these costs as an investment in your family's peace of mind.

The Bottom Line

Every young adult who owns property, has assets, or is responsible for dependents needs a will. But don't stop there. Adding trusts, powers of attorney, and healthcare directives ensures you are fully prepared. It doesn't matter if your "estate" is a car, a savings account, or a cherished collection of Pokémon cards—your documents ensure your wishes are respected.

A will and related estate documents give you control, protect your loved ones, allow you to provide gifts, and secure the care of your children. Creating them is a responsible, practical step that provides peace of mind to both you and your family.

And remember—this information is meant for educational purposes. Laws differ from state to state, and your situation is unique. Always consult with an attorney or qualified professional for legal advice about wills, trusts, and estate planning.

Start now—your family, and your future self, will thank you.

Favorite Points and Notes

Chapter Four

Fitness

Fitness

First Things First

"Strength doesn't come from what you can do; it comes from overcoming the things you once thought you couldn't." – Rikki Rogers

They say the early bird gets the worm — but what they don't mention is that not everyone is the same kind of bird. Some people thrive before dawn, while others hit their stride when the sun is higher in the sky. The truth is that success doesn't belong to those who rise the earliest; it belongs to those who rise *with purpose*.

This isn't a message on waking up at 5:00 a.m. or cold plunging into an ice bath before sunrise. It's about something much more simple and far more powerful — **starting your day with clarity, consistency, and care.** The way you greet the morning determines how you'll handle the hours that follow. Whether your day begins at 6 a.m. or 8 a.m., what matters most is that you begin it *intentionally*.

What if you *are* an early riser? That's great too. If you feel most creative or productive before the world wakes up, embrace it! The goal isn't to convince you to change your natural body clock — it's to help you tune in to the rhythm that helps *you* perform your best. Some people's focus peaks at dawn, others at mid-morning or even later in the day. What matters is that you *know yourself* and show up for your day with consistency, focus, and intention.

The Energy You Bring to the Day

Your morning is the doorway to your day — a fresh start every twenty-four hours. The thoughts you think, the emotions you allow, and the actions you take in those first waking moments quietly set the tone for everything that follows.

If you begin your day scrolling, rushing, or reacting, your mind stays in that frantic state. But if you start with intention — a few deep breaths, a little movement, and gratitude for the chance to begin again — you anchor yourself in control.

It's not about perfection; it's about presence.

Each day is a blank page. What you write on it begins the moment you open your eyes.

Ask Yourself:

- What's the first thing I want to *feel* this morning — calm, motivated, grateful, confident?
- What's one thing I can do right now to create that feeling?

Work with Your Own Rhythm

Some people naturally feel alert before sunrise. Others think most clearly once the world is fully awake. You know yourself better than any productivity article ever could.

If your internal clock doesn't match society's early-bird schedule, don't force it. Starting your day intentionally doesn't mean starting it *unnaturally early.* It means respecting your rhythm while still respecting your responsibilities.

That said, lying in bed until midmorning, mindlessly scrolling or avoiding the day, won't bring the results you want. There's a difference between honoring your internal pace and avoiding life.

Find your balance — that sweet spot where your energy, creativity, and focus align. Some people's peak hours are early morning, others are late morning or even evening. The goal isn't to mimic someone else's routine, but to master your own.

When you understand how you function best, you can build habits that fit *you*. That's when consistency feels natural instead of forced.

Reflection Prompts:

- When do I feel most alert and creative — morning, afternoon, or evening?
- Am I using that time wisely or wasting it on distractions?
- What time feels like a healthy, realistic start to my day — one I can commit to regularly?

The Three Pillars of a Strong Morning

A balanced morning sets the stage for a balanced life. To create that balance, focus on three key pillars that build a strong foundation for the day ahead:
Mental fitness, emotional fitness, and physical fitness.

You'll explore these areas in greater depth later, but let's look at how they intertwine in your morning routine.

1. Mental Fitness: Waking Up Your Mind

Your mental state at the start of your day determines how you process everything that follows. It's not just what you do, but how you *think* while doing it.

Before the emails, the errands, or the endless notifications — pause. Take a few quiet moments to collect your thoughts.

Instead of reaching for your phone, reach for stillness. Sit up, stretch, and ask yourself a few grounding questions:

- What matters most to me today?
- What one thing will make this day feel productive or meaningful?
- How do I want to show up for myself and others?

This simple reflection — two minutes, no journal required — helps you direct your focus before the world starts pulling it in a hundred directions.

Try adding a short ritual that engages your mind positively: reading something inspiring, writing a few lines in a gratitude journal, or listening to music that lifts your mood. Your brain wakes up best when it's fed thoughtful input, not stress or noise.

When you start your morning with intention instead of reaction, you stop letting life happen *to* you and start shaping it *with* you.

2. Emotional Fitness: Grounding Yourself Before the Day Begins

How you feel when you wake up often predicts how you'll respond to challenges later. If you start anxious or overwhelmed, small frustrations will feel like mountains. But if you begin centered and calm, you'll face the day with emotional steadiness.

Emotional fitness means checking in with yourself before checking on everything else.

Take a breath and notice what's going on internally. You don't need to "fix" your feelings — just acknowledge them. Maybe you're excited, maybe you're worried, maybe you're tired. Awareness is the first step toward balance.

You might find it helpful to take a few quiet minutes for prayer, meditation, or journaling. Write down three things you're grateful for or one thing you're looking forward to. Gratitude doesn't erase stress, but it reminds you that life still holds good things, even on tough mornings.

And if your morning starts rough — you wake up late, spill your coffee, or feel off — don't let it define your entire day. Reset. Breathe. Start again. You can always choose a different attitude.

Try This:
Each morning, finish this sentence in your mind:

"Today, I choose to…"
It might be "Today, I choose to stay calm," or "Today, I choose to give my best," or "Today, I choose joy."
Whatever it is, let it guide you through the hours ahead.

3. Physical Fitness: Moving Your Body to Wake Your Energy

Your body and mind are deeply connected. Physical movement doesn't just strengthen muscles — it clears your thoughts, lifts your mood, and jump-starts motivation.

You don't need a two-hour gym session or a marathon. A few minutes of movement each morning can make a world of difference.

Take a brisk walk, stretch your arms, or put on music and dance while you make breakfast. Movement tells your brain, *We're awake. We're ready.*

Think of your body as an engine — it performs best when it's warm, fueled, and cared for. Movement increases blood flow, improves focus, and triggers the release of endorphins that make you feel good.

If mornings are hard for you, keep it simple. Do something small, but do it consistently. It's better to move for five minutes every day than for an hour once a week.

And remember, your body deserves gratitude, not criticism. Exercise because you appreciate it, not because you're punishing it.

Building a Morning That Works for You

There's no perfect formula, no one-size-fits-all schedule. A great morning routine is simply one that *works for you.*

Maybe that means:

- Waking at 6:30 a.m. for a quiet cup of coffee before the world stirs.
- Starting at 7:00 a.m. with a walk or light stretch.
- Or even beginning at 8:00 a.m. after a restful, focused night of creative work.

Whatever time you choose, treat those first waking minutes as sacred. Protect them from chaos and distraction. Use them to align your mind, emotions, and body. If you begin your day with intention — no matter the hour — you'll find yourself more focused, resilient, and ready to handle whatever comes your way.

Morning Alignment Prompts:

- What's one small habit I can do every morning to anchor my day?
- How can I use my first ten minutes to strengthen my mental, emotional, or physical fitness?
- What time feels like *my* best starting point for a productive day?

Sample Morning Routines:

Everyone's schedule and rhythm look different — and that's okay. The goal isn't to copy someone else's plan; it's to design a routine that fits your life and your energy.

Early Riser Routine (starts around 5:30–6:00 a.m.) – 90 minutes

- 5:30 a.m. – Wake up, drink a glass of water, and open the curtains to let in natural light.
- 5:40 a.m. – Light stretching, yoga, or a 20-minute walk outside.
- 6:00 a.m. – Meditate and a short journaling session.
- 6:20 a.m. – Read or listen to something inspiring for 15 minutes.
- 6:40 a.m. – Shower, breakfast, and prepare for the day.
- 7:00 a.m. – Begin work, study, or creative projects.

Mid-Morning Routine (starts around 7:00–7:30 a.m.) – 60 minutes

- 7:00 a.m. – Wake up, hydrate, and stretch for 5–10 minutes.
- 7:15 a.m. – Eat a healthy breakfast or smoothie.
- 7:30 a.m. – Take a quick walk or do 10 minutes of body movement.
- 7:45 a.m. – Read, pray, or write down your top three goals for the day.
- 8:00 a.m. – Shower, get ready, and start your day's priorities.

Later Starter Routine (starts around 8:00–8:30 a.m.) – 30–45 minutes

- 8:00 a.m. – Wake up, drink water, and open windows or step outside for sunlight.
- 8:10 a.m. – Quick stretches or a short burst of movement (dance, jumping jacks, squats).
- 8:20 a.m. – Enjoy a healthy breakfast while reading something uplifting.
- 8:40 a.m. – Review your plan for the day and set your focus.
- 9:00 a.m. – Begin your work or studies with clarity and calm.

There's no wrong option — only what works for your body, lifestyle, and energy. The point is consistency, not comparison.

Let Go of Comparison

You might see endless videos or posts of "high achievers" who claim to get up at 4:45 a.m., run five miles, meditate for thirty minutes, and read two chapters before breakfast. That may work for them, but it doesn't have to work for you.

Don't let someone else's schedule make you feel inadequate. Discipline is important, but so is self-awareness. You can live a productive, meaningful life without following a formula designed for someone else's body and brain.

What matters is consistency — not comparison. If you start your day every morning at 7:00 a.m., focused and ready, that's far more powerful than waking at 5:00 a.m. and hitting snooze three times out of exhaustion.

Your rhythm, your pace, your goals — that's where the magic happens.

A Day Built on Intention

Starting your day right isn't about creating a rigid routine. It's about setting a tone — one of focus, gratitude, and movement.

When you begin your morning intentionally, you build momentum for the hours ahead. Small wins — like drinking water, stretching, or making your bed — signal to your brain that you're capable and in control. Those early victories stack into larger ones throughout the day.

The goal isn't to do *everything*; it's to do the *right things* for you. The habits that ground you mentally, emotionally, and physically.

At the end of the day, fitness isn't just about muscle tone or endurance — it's about alignment. A fit life begins in the mind, steadies in the heart, and strengthens in the body. When those three are connected, you feel balanced, confident, and capable.

Start your mornings as an act of self-respect. Honor your time, your energy, and your rhythm. Don't rush. Don't compare. Don't coast. Just begin intentionally, honestly, and fully awake to the life waiting for you.

At-a-Glance Reflection: "First Things First"

- You don't need a 5:00 a.m. alarm to succeed — you need *focus*.
- Build your morning around mental clarity, emotional balance, and physical movement.
- Respect your natural rhythm — early, mid, or late — and stay consistent.
- Replace comparison with commitment.
- Treat the first hour of your day as the foundation for everything that follows.

Favorite Points and Notes

Mental Fitness
Training Your Mind

What does it take to truly thrive in life—not just survive the daily grind, not just get by, but actually grow, feel steady, capable, and at peace within yourself? What is it to live with purpose?

When we say fitness, most people focus on physical health — nutrition, exercise, sleep, stronger muscles, better endurance, more energy—but we often overlook the part that directs everything else: the mind. The mind deserves the same level of care and training as your body. Your mental strength determines how well you handle your work, your relationships, your stress, your dreams. Your mental fitness determines how you think, respond, and recover when life throws you curveballs. It's the foundation that helps you make clear decisions and maintain emotional balance. Mental fitness is not just about feeling okay; it's about training your thoughts, attitudes, and emotions so that you can handle whatever life throws your way with strength and clarity.

Think of mental fitness as physical fitness for your brain. Being mentally fit doesn't mean you'll never struggle or stumble. It means you've built the strength, flexibility, and resilience to face challenges with confidence rather than fear. Just as your physical fitness improves when you consistently challenge your body, your mental fitness grows when you intentionally train your mind. The intentional practice of building resilience, clarity, flexibility, and focus—so you can show up as your best self, even on hard days.

Mental fitness is not about perfection or pretending life is easy. It's about creating a strong internal foundation that helps you stay steady through life's ups and downs.

What Is Mental Fitness?

Mental fitness is your ability to think clearly, regulate emotions, and make wise decisions even under stress. It's your resilience, adaptability, and self-awareness all working together to help you live intentionally instead of reactively.

It's the proactive approach — developing habits and perspectives that keep your mind sharp, flexible, and positive.

You wouldn't wait until your muscles completely gave out before starting to exercise, and you shouldn't wait until your mind is overwhelmed before you strengthen it.

In essence, **mental fitness means having the tools and habits that help you think well, feel well, and live well.**

Why Mental Fitness Matters

Life is full of highs and lows, wins and losses, surprises and setbacks. You can't predict every challenge, but you can prepare your mind to face them. Life is unpredictable. No one is exempt from disappointment, change, or uncertainty. When you're mentally fit, those moments don't define you — they refine you.

Building mental fitness helps you handle stress, recover faster from emotional setbacks, and approach life with a calm and confident mindset. It's about being proactive, not reactive—creating a foundation strong enough to carry you through whatever comes your way.

Building mental fitness helps you:

- **Reduce stress** by improving how you process and respond to challenges.
- **Stay focused** and productive even when life feels chaotic.

- **Think clearly** when emotions run high.
- **Recover faster** from setbacks.
- **Build stronger relationships** through patience, empathy, and good communication.

When you're mentally fit, you're not just surviving the day. You're steering it. You think more clearly, respond more thoughtfully, and act in ways that align with your values. Ultimately, mental fitness allows you to thrive instead of just survive. It helps you become the kind of person who can say, "This is tough, but I can handle it."

The Difference Between Mental Health and Mental Fitness

Let's start with a simple distinction.
Mental health is your overall state of emotional, psychological, and social well-being. It's how you feel, think, and relate to the world.

Mental fitness, on the other hand, is the active practice of strengthening your mind. It's the daily training you do—just like physical exercise—to build resilience, focus, optimism, and adaptability.

Think of it this way: mental health is the condition of your mind, and mental fitness is the routine that keeps it strong. One is the state; the other is the strategy. Where *mental health* is your overall state of well-being, *mental fitness* is the daily practice of building it. Mental health is your condition, while mental fitness is your workout routine. One is the state you want to protect; the other is how you get there.

When you approach your mind as something that can be trained, you stop seeing your emotions and reactions as fixed traits and start seeing them as muscles you can strengthen. That mindset alone changes everything.

Imagine two people facing the same stressful event. One reacts impulsively, feels defeated, and struggles to regain focus. The other takes a deep breath, reflects, seeks perspective, and calmly works toward a solution. The second person isn't immune to stress—they're simply *mentally fit*. They've trained for it.

But being mentally fit doesn't mean you're happy all the time; it means you have the agility to recover faster, think more clearly, and stay true to your values when life tests you.

Where *mental health* refers to your overall state of wellbeing, *mental fitness* is the work you do to maintain and strengthen it. Think of it as the difference between *being healthy* and *training to stay strong*.

Training the Mind Like a Muscle

Mental fitness doesn't happen overnight. It's built through small, consistent habits that strengthen your thoughts, emotions, and behaviors.

If physical training builds endurance in your body, mental training builds endurance in your perspective. It gives you the capacity to adapt, to stay grounded when life gets uncertain, and to recover after you've been stretched thin.

The mind is flexible, thanks to a phenomenon called **neuroplasticity**—your brain's ability to grow and rewire itself. Each time you practice patience instead of anger, focus instead of distraction, or optimism instead of fear, you're literally reshaping your brain. You're training it to default to strength instead of stress.

Mental fitness isn't about avoiding struggle—it's about meeting it with stability and clarity. It's what helps you bend without breaking.

You don't wait until your muscles weaken before you exercise them, and the same should go for your mind. Mental fitness helps you navigate challenges with a clear head and calm heart. Life will always include stress, setbacks, and change, but how you respond—that's what defines your growth.

Developing mental fitness means training yourself to pause before reacting, to see problems as opportunities to adapt, and to trust your ability to recover. It helps you bounce back from disappointment, handle uncertainty, and find meaning in the process. Over time, you build endurance for life's ups and downs, and that endurance turns into confidence.

When you prioritize your mental fitness, you learn to manage emotions without being overwhelmed by them. You strengthen your focus, your self-awareness, and your capacity to stay grounded in difficult moments. It's not about becoming unshakable; it's about learning how to bend without breaking.

The Foundations of Mental Fitness: Everyday Practices.

The best way to strengthen your mental fitness is through daily habits. Just like physical training, consistency is key. You don't need grand gestures or complicated plans — just intentional actions that support your growth.

You can think of mental fitness as a combination of interconnected practices—skills you can develop over time to build a strong and balanced mindset.

1. Live Mindfully

Mindfulness isn't about emptying your mind or living in silence. It's about paying attention—to your thoughts, your surroundings, and your reactions—without judgment. When you're mindful, you slow down enough to notice what's happening right now instead of getting lost in what-ifs or regrets. Simple practices like deep breathing, short meditations, journaling, or even mindful walking can retrain your brain to stay calm and focused.

2. Challenge Your Thoughts

Your mind is always talking — make sure it's saying something true. Learn to recognize when you're telling yourself negative or exaggerated stories. Question your thoughts: *Is this fact or fear?* Replace "I can't" with "I'm learning." Replace "I failed" with "I tried and I'll try again."

3. Embrace Flexible Thinking

Life rarely goes according to plan. Flexible thinking helps you adapt when things shift unexpectedly. It means viewing obstacles as puzzles to solve rather than proof that you've failed.
Try reframing challenges by asking, *"What can I learn from this?"* or *"How else can I approach this?"*—that's how growth begins.

4. Keep Learning

Read new books, explore new topics, try new hobbies. Learning keeps your brain engaged and adaptable. Every time you step outside your comfort zone, you build new neural pathways that keep your mind strong and flexible.

5. Act Purposefully

Purpose gives direction to your days and meaning to your efforts. It's not about having every detail of life figured out—it's about aligning what you do with what you care about.
Take time to reflect on your values, your strengths, and

what brings you joy. When your actions reflect your purpose, your life feels balanced and fulfilling.

6. Take Mental Breaks

Your brain needs rest just like your body does. Pause between tasks. Step outside. Breathe deeply. These little resets help prevent burnout and boost creativity.

7. Recharge Your Body

A clear mind lives in a healthy body. Sleep, movement, and relaxation aren't luxuries—they're mental necessities. When you're exhausted or over-stimulated, your ability to focus, regulate emotions, and make good decisions declines.
Commit to getting enough rest, eating foods that truly fuel you, and moving daily in whatever way brings you joy. Remember: mental energy and physical energy rise and fall together.

8. Build Emotional Endurance

When challenges arise, don't push your feelings away. Acknowledge them. Name what you're feeling and then choose how to respond. This is emotional regulation — the ability to stay grounded when life feels unstable

Living Mindfully: Strengthening Awareness

Mental fitness begins with awareness.
Before you can change your reactions or build better habits, you have to notice what's happening inside your mind.

Mindfulness is one of the most powerful tools for this. It's the art of slowing down, observing your thoughts and feelings without judgment, and grounding yourself in the present moment.

When you're mindful, you give yourself space between what happens and how you respond. That small pause—just a breath or two—can make all the difference between reacting impulsively and responding wisely.

You can practice mindfulness anywhere: while brushing your teeth, walking, eating, or even driving. It's not about clearing your mind; it's about noticing it.

Try This:
When you feel your thoughts racing, pause for a moment and ask yourself, *"What am I thinking right now?"* Don't judge it—just notice. Awareness is the first step to control.

Living mindfully trains your mind to stay present, and when your mind is present, your decisions and relationships follow suit.

Flexible Thinking: The Art of Adaptability

Have you ever noticed that some people crumble under change, while others seem to roll with it?
The difference often lies in *mental flexibility.*

Flexible thinking means being able to adapt when things don't go as planned. It's shifting your perspective, finding new solutions, and choosing curiosity over frustration.

When you're mentally fit, you understand that your first thought isn't always your best thought. You're open to exploring new ideas, questioning your assumptions, and trying again when something fails.

This skill keeps you from getting stuck in negative patterns or rigid beliefs. It helps you solve problems creatively and stay calm in uncertainty.

Just like stretching keeps your body from injury, mental flexibility keeps your mind from breaking under pressure.

Try This:
Next time something doesn't go your way, ask:

- *What else could this mean?*
- *What can I learn from this?*
- *How can I see this situation differently?*

That small mental shift is how growth begins.

Connection and Community: You're Not in This Alone

Mental fitness isn't something you build in isolation. While many of your habits are personal—journaling, reflecting, practicing mindfulness—your growth is deeply connected to the people around you. We're wired for connection. It's what grounds us when life gets messy and reminds us that we're never walking alone.

When you surround yourself with positive, supportive people, you multiply your resilience. Healthy relationships act as anchors in the unpredictable waves of life. They give you the courage to face hard days and the comfort of knowing someone has your back. In fact, studies show that people who maintain strong social bonds recover faster from stress, experience lower levels of depression, and even live longer, happier lives.

Being mentally fit means knowing when to lean in and when to reach out. It's the courage to say, *"I need help,"* and the empathy to ask, *"How are you really doing?"* True strength isn't about doing everything alone; it's about recognizing that connection amplifies your ability to thrive.

Your support system can include family, friends, mentors, or professionals who help you see life through a wider lens. Sometimes a five-minute talk with someone who listens without judgment can restore perspective better than hours of overthinking.

It's also about being the kind of person others can rely on—offering encouragement, listening deeply, and showing up with authenticity. The energy you bring to your relationships circles back in powerful ways. When you lift others, you lift yourself too.

So, nurture your relationships like the living things they are. Call your friends just to check in. Have dinner with your family without the distraction of screens. Be fully present when someone shares something important. Every genuine interaction adds strength to your emotional foundation.

Connection and community are not just parts of mental fitness—they're its heartbeat. The journey to a stronger mind is meant to be shared. Together, we heal faster, learn more, and find the courage to keep moving forward.

Reflection Prompt:
Who in your life helps you grow, listen, and stay grounded? How can you strengthen that connection this week?

Purpose: The Fuel for Resilience

A strong mind doesn't just handle challenges—it understands *why* it's worth facing them.

Your sense of purpose is what gives meaning to your days, especially when things get hard. It's the "why" behind your effort, the reason you get up and keep going even when motivation fades.

Finding your purpose isn't about having one grand mission; it's about discovering what truly matters to you—your values, strengths, and passions—and aligning your actions with them.

Purpose gives you direction when you feel lost, stability when life feels unstable, and courage when you're uncertain.

Try This:
Write down three things that give your life meaning. Maybe it's family, creativity, service, or personal growth.
Then ask: *How can I include more of this in my day-to-day life?*

Living with purpose isn't about perfection—it's about alignment. It's about knowing who you are and showing up for that version of yourself every single day.

Recharge: Resting the Mind to Stay Strong

You can't pour from an empty cup.
Even the strongest minds need recovery time.

Resting your mind isn't laziness—it's maintenance. When you give yourself permission to step back, you allow your brain to restore focus, regulate emotions, and boost creativity.

Sleep, quiet time, hobbies, laughter—these aren't luxuries; they're part of the training plan.

Schedule downtime the same way you schedule work or workouts. Take breaks from screens, spend time in nature, or simply breathe deeply and reset.

Remember:
You can't be mentally fit if you're constantly exhausted. Rest is the bridge between effort and strength.

Guarding Your Mind: Be Careful What You Feed It

We live in a world that's louder than ever. Everyone has an opinion, every headline is urgent, and every scroll brings a new voice telling you what to think, who to trust, and how to feel. Unfortunately, we've reached a point where disagreeing with someone often leads to being accused of being "brainwashed." But the truth is, your mind is one of the most impressionable and powerful tools you have—and what you feed it determines how it grows.

Be very careful what you listen to and what you believe. Your mind doesn't just absorb information; it accepts it as truth when repeated often enough. It doesn't know the difference between what's true and what's simply *familiar*. That's why it's essential to pause, to question, and to reflect before you accept anything as fact. Ask yourself: *Does this align with my core values? Does it reflect honesty and reason? Or is it feeding fear, anger, and division?*

Your thoughts are shaped by what you take in—news, entertainment, conversations, social media, even teachers, bosses and the people closest to you. If you don't intentionally protect your mind, it's easy for negativity or misinformation to seep in and quietly shape your worldview. You can't always control what's around you, but you can control what you allow to stay in your mind.

Feed your mind truth. Feed it common sense. Feed it love. Feed it honesty. Feed it your faith and your beliefs. Choose to fill your thoughts with what uplifts, not what tears down.

When you protect what enters your mind, you protect your peace. And that peace becomes the foundation for your mental strength, your emotional balance, and your moral clarity. Guard your thoughts carefully—they will shape the person you become.

The Comparison Trap: Protecting Your Mind in the Age of Social Media

In a world of highlight reels and filters, it's easy to lose perspective. Social media was meant to connect us, but too often it does the opposite—it turns connection into quiet competition. What begins as a few minutes of scrolling can quietly turn into self-doubt. You see someone's vacation, their promotion, their perfectly curated home, and suddenly your own life feels smaller. It happens fast, and the emotional impact is real. The more we compare, the more we chip away at our peace of mind, feeding anxiety, envy, and an ongoing sense that we're somehow behind.

The truth is, most of what we see online is not reality—it's a polished version of it. For every perfect photo there's a pile of stress, sacrifice, or struggle that never makes it to the screen. When we forget that, our mental fitness suffers. Confidence turns to questioning, joy fades into jealousy, and we start to believe that our worth depends on how well we measure up. But comparison doesn't build strength; it drains it.

Breaking free doesn't mean disappearing from the digital world—it means reclaiming control. You get to decide what you consume and how it shapes your thoughts. Curate your feed so it uplifts instead of undermines you. Follow accounts that educate, encourage, or make you laugh. Limit the noise that triggers insecurity, and remind yourself that someone else's success is not your failure. Gratitude, mindfulness, and presence are the antidotes to comparison.

The more you protect your mental space, the more you realize this simple truth: comparison is optional. Your life doesn't need to look like anyone else's to be meaningful. It already matters because it's yours. So, the next time you find yourself scrolling and spiraling, pause and remember—you don't need to measure up, you just need to show up for your own life. That's where real confidence and lasting joy begin.

Daily Habits for a Stronger Mind

Just like physical exercise, consistency matters more than intensity. Here are simple, daily habits that strengthen your mind:

- **Challenge your thoughts.** Not every thought is true or helpful. Ask yourself, *"Is this fact or fear?"*
- **Train your focus.** Try short bursts of meditation or mindful breathing to strengthen attention.
- **Create routines and rituals.** Structure calms the mind and reduces decision fatigue.
- **Limit digital noise.** Protect your focus by setting boundaries with social media and screens.
- **Keep learning.** New experiences build new neural pathways—learn an instrument, take a class, or read something that stretches your thinking.
- **Practice gratitude.** Write down three things you're thankful for daily to retrain your brain toward optimism.
- **Let go of control.** Focus on what you can change; release what you can't.
- **Rest your mind.** Give yourself permission to pause without guilt. True rest refuels creativity and clarity.
- **Move your body.** Even a ten-minute walk can sharpen focus and lift your mood. Physical activity is one of the most powerful mood boosters available.
- **Listen inward.** Your intuition often knows what your mind tries to ignore.

- **Celebrate small wins.** Every mental victory counts—acknowledge it.
- **Breathe deeply.** When you're overwhelmed, pause and take three slow, full breaths.
- **Reflect regularly.** Take time each week to think about what's working in your life and what's draining you.
- **Connect with others.** Build friendships that inspire and challenge you.
- **Let go of perfection.** Aim for progress, not flawless performance.

These habits are like mental push-ups. The more consistently you practice them, the stronger your mind becomes.

The Role of Resilience

Resilience is the heart of mental fitness. It's what allows you to bounce back after hardship and find meaning in adversity.

A resilient mind doesn't deny pain—it learns from it. It uses obstacles as opportunities to grow stronger and wiser.

You build resilience through practice: by facing challenges, reflecting on them, and realizing you survived. Each time you do, you strengthen your belief that you can handle what's next.

Resilience turns "I can't" into "I can learn." It transforms stress into growth and fear into courage.

The Long-Term Payoff

When you build mental fitness, life doesn't necessarily get easier—but *you* get stronger. You'll notice the difference in subtle, powerful ways. When you commit to mental fitness, you invest in a lifetime of benefits:

- You think more clearly under pressure.
- You handle change with grace instead of panic.
- You build relationships that are stronger and more authentic.
- You recover faster from stress, setbacks, and disappointment.
- You live with purpose and clarity, not confusion and chaos.

You'll notice these benefits gradually, just as you would after consistent physical training. Some days you'll feel the progress; other days, you'll just trust the process. But over time, you'll realize you've built something powerful—a mind that doesn't just survive but thrives. You'll become less reactive, more intentional, and more peaceful in how you live.

- You'll respond instead of react.
- You'll pause before spiraling.
- You'll forgive yourself faster and judge yourself less.
- You'll see solutions where you used to see problems.
- You'll find peace in progress, not perfection.

Mentally fit people don't avoid discomfort; they work through it with self-awareness, humility, and courage. They understand that growth and struggle are part of the same process—and they face both with grace.

- Stop taking every negative comment personally.
- Recover faster from disappointment.
- Notice small joys that used to go unseen.
- Have more patience with others — and with yourself.
- Feel clearer about your purpose and more confident in your direction.

When your mind is fit, your life reflects it. You make decisions that align with your values. You stop living on autopilot and start showing up with purpose.

Final Thoughts

Your mind is your most powerful muscle. Treat it like one. Feed it well, challenge it often, and rest it regularly. Mental fitness is not a one-time achievement. It's a lifelong commitment to your own growth. Some days you'll feel strong and centered; other days you'll feel scattered and tired. That's normal. What matters most is that you keep showing up for yourself.

Mental fitness isn't about avoiding problems; it's about facing them with strength, wisdom, and peace. It's about knowing that even when life gets hard, *you're equipped to handle it.* Mental fitness is an act of self-respect. It's the daily commitment to nurture the one instrument you use for everything else in life—your mind. Just as your muscles strengthen with use, your thoughts, focus, and emotional resilience grow stronger the more you train them. Your thoughts create your direction. Your habits shape your confidence. And your focus determines your future.

As you grow in this area, remember: there's no finish line. There's only progress.
Each day you choose awareness, gratitude, learning, or connection, you're building your mental strength one small rep at a time. The key is to start small, stay consistent, and be kind to yourself along the way. Some days you'll feel strong and centered; other days you'll feel stretched thin—and both are okay. What matters is that you keep showing up. Train your mind like it matters—because it does. When you build your mental fitness, you build the foundation for everything else: your relationships, your career, your happiness, and your peace.

Stay patient with yourself. Stay curious about your growth. Stay compassionate with your journey. You can't control every challenge life throws your way, but you *can* control how you prepare, how you respond, and how you rebuild. Mental fitness is your lifelong practice for doing exactly that.

Favorite Points and Notes

Emotional Fitness
Strong Heart, Steady Life

When most people hear "fitness," they think cardio, meal prep, maybe a mindfulness app. Emotional fitness is the part that often gets skipped, yet it is what keeps you steady when life tilts. Emotional fitness is your capacity to notice what you feel, name it clearly, regulate it wisely, and respond in ways that move your life forward. It is not about never feeling sad, angry, or anxious. It is about building the strength, awareness, and skills to handle those feelings without letting them drive the car.

If physical fitness trains your body and mental fitness trains your mind, emotional fitness trains your heart's habits. The goal is not perfection. The goal is resilience, clarity, and peace under pressure.

What Emotional Fitness Really Means

Think of emotional fitness as four interlocking skills:

1. **Awareness, noticing without judgment.**
   You pay attention to your inner signals the way a good driver watches the dashboard. You see the "check engine" light early.
2. **Naming, putting feelings into words.**
   When you can say, I feel disappointed and a little scared, your brain shifts from raw reactivity to problem-solving. Words create space.
3. **Regulation, calming your nervous system.**
   You know how to downshift your body with breath, routine, and boundaries so your emotions do not run you.

4. **Response, choosing aligned actions.**
   You act according to your values, not according to your worst moment. You make it to the gym even after a rough day. You apologize without a five-paragraph defense. You walk away when needed.

This is a training plan for your inner life. With practice, your emotional stamina grows.

The Myths That Keep You From Training

Myth 1, "Strong people do not feel big feelings."
Reality, strong people feel everything and still choose wise actions. Strength includes tears, laughter, and honest words.

Myth 2, "If I acknowledge a feeling, it will take over."
Reality, ignored feelings leak out sideways. Named feelings calm down faster.

Myth 3, "I should be over this by now."
Reality, healing is not linear. Progress is measured in better choices and faster recoveries, not in never being triggered again.

Myth 4, "Other people cause my emotions."
Reality, people and events influence you, your interpretation and response shape your emotional experience. That is power, not blame.

Your Core Tools

1) Name it to tame it

A simple sentence is your best starter tool, I feel ___ because ___. Example, I feel anxious because the exam is close and I have not reviewed Chapter 6. This moves you from "everything is scary" to "do Chapter 6."

Mini-exercise, the 3-Word Check
Three times today, pause and write three words, one emotion, one need, one action.

- Emotion, frustrated.
- Need, clarity.
- Action, email the professor with two specific questions.

2) Breathe like you mean it

Your breath is a remote control for your nervous system. Longer exhales calm the body.

Protocol, 4-4-6
Inhale four, hold four, exhale six. Repeat for sixty to ninety seconds. This is your in-the-moment reset before you send the text, speak in the meeting, or step on the court.

3) Move the feeling through

Emotions are physical. A brisk walk, pushups against the wall, or a stretch sequence helps metabolize stress hormones. Motion changes emotion.

Try this
Two minutes of marching in place, ten slow squats, twenty shoulder rolls. Now re-assess the problem.

4) Create a "calm kit"

When your mind is loud, decision-making gets sloppy. Your calm kit is a small list you do in order without debate.

Example calm kit

- Drink water.
- 4-4-6 breathing for ninety seconds.
- Write the 3-Word Check.

- One five-minute tidy or walk.
- One text to a safe person, "Hard morning, taking a reset, calling at six."

5) Rewrite the story

Your first thought is often a survival script. Challenge it.

Reframe your script

- Thought, I always mess up.
- Evidence, I passed last semester, I prepared, I asked for feedback.
- New story, This is hard and I am improving. My job is effort and adjustment.

The Five Emotions You Will See Most, and How to Train Them

1) Anxiety, energy without direction

- **What it says,** something might go wrong.
- **Train it,** shrink your time horizon. Focus on the next honest step.
- **Tool,** the two-column plan. Column A, worries. Column B, tiny actions. Do one from B now.

2) Anger, protector of values

- **What it says,** a boundary was crossed or a value was violated.
- **Train it,** slow your body before you speak. Decide if this needs a conversation, a boundary, or a change in expectation.
- **Tool,** the boundary sentence, I care about you, I am not okay with ___, here is what I will do.

3) Sadness, signal for processing and rest

- **What it says,** something mattered and it is missing.
- **Train it,** make space to feel, then choose one nourishing action.
- **Tool,** the two letters you will not send, one raw, one calm. Shred the first, save the second if you need a future script.

4) Guilt, course-corrector

- **What it says,** you did something out of alignment.
- **Train it,** repair quickly.
- **Tool,** the four Rs, **recognize** the harm, **responsibility** with no excuses, **repair** with a concrete action, **relearn** the boundary that prevents a repeat.

5) Shame, identity threat

- **What it says,** you are the mistake.
- **Train it,** bring it to a safe person and to the truth.
- **Tool,** the compassion script, I did X, it does not define me. I can make amends and learn. I am still worthy of respect.

Emotional Fitness at School, Work, and Home

At school

- Use office hours as a regulation tool. Preparing two questions reduces exam panic.
- Study in ninety-minute blocks with a five-minute reset, water, breath, stretch.
- After a bad grade, run the four Rs within twenty-four hours.

At work

- Before difficult conversations, write your boundary sentence and your desired outcome.
- When nervous, practice your opening line aloud three times.
- After a mistake, send a short repair email, what happened, what I am doing to fix it, what I will do differently next time.

At home

- Use a family or roommate "yellow flag" phrase, I need ten minutes to cool down. Return at a set time.
- Have a weekly thirty-minute life admin block, budget check, appointment scheduling, small repairs. Reduces background stress.

Relationships and Emotional Fitness

Emotionally fit relationships have three rhythms:

1. **Clear bids for connection**
   You reach out on purpose, dinner Tuesday, call after class, quick walk. Waiting for perfect moments kills connection.
2. **Repair attempts**
   All relationships rupture. Healthy ones repair quickly. I snapped earlier, I was stressed. I am sorry. Can we try that again.
3. **Boundary clarity**
   You protect the relationship by protecting yourselves. I want to support you, I cannot text during work, I will respond after six.

Two-minute exercise, the Relationship Audit
List three people who lift you and three who drain you. Plan one touch with the lifters this week. Set one boundary with a drainer, kindly and clearly.

Social Media and Emotional Load

Your feed becomes your emotional diet. If your inputs are outrage and comparison, your emotions will reflect it.

- Curate ruthlessly. Mute accounts that inflame rather than inform.
- Use time boxes. Fifteen minutes, timer on.
- Add "mindful follows" that educate, inspire, or teach skills.
- Replace one scroll a day with a walk, a call, or a page of a good book.

Sleep, Food, and Movement, The Emotional Multiplier

Your feelings ride on your physiology. Low sleep, high sugar, and zero movement will make any emotion bigger and harder to handle.

Anchor routine

- Water on waking.
- Movement for ten minutes daily.
- Protein and fiber at breakfast when you can.
- Lights down one hour before bed.
- Same sleep window most nights.

This is not about perfection. It is about giving your emotions a stable platform.

Communication Under Pressure

Use this two-step approach when you are heated.

1. **Reflect,** I feel ___ because ___. What I want is ___.
2. **Request,** Would you be willing to ___ so we can___.

Example
I feel overwhelmed because the chores pile up by Sunday. What I want is a simple plan. Would you be willing to try a twenty-minute clean on Friday night so we can enjoy Saturday.

Short sentences. Calm voice. One clear ask.

A 7-Day Emotional Fitness Sprint

Try this as an on-ramp.

- **Day 1, Name it.** 3-Word Check, morning, noon, evening.
- **Day 2, Breathe it.** 4-4-6 before every important task.
- **Day 3, Move it.** Ten minutes of movement after a stressful moment.
- **Day 4, Boundaries.** Write and practice one boundary sentence.
- **Day 5, Repair.** Use the four Rs for one small mistake.
- **Day 6, Connect.** Send two encouragement texts, ask one honest question in a conversation.
- **Day 7, Reflect.** Journal five lines, what improved, what surprised me, what I will keep next week.

Repeat as needed. Keep it simple and repeatable.

Rebuilding After an Emotional Hit

When life sideswipes you, focus on four stabilizers:

1. **Safety,** clear your calendar where possible, lean on safe people, sleep and food first.
2. **Story,** write a one-page account of what happened, with facts only, then a second page for feelings and meanings.

3. **Structure,** simple daily anchors, wake time, water, movement, one priority task.
4. **Support,** ask for professional help if your daily function drops or you feel stuck. Getting help is an emotionally fit choice.

The Comparison Trap

Comparison is one of the fastest ways to sabotage emotional stability. You do not see people's full context, only their highlights.

- Limit inputs that trigger envy.
- Replace "Why not me" with "What is one step I can take today," then do it.
- Practice gratitude with specifics, three lines nightly.

Gratitude does not deny pain. It keeps your attention from being held hostage by it.

Your Emotional Fitness Scorecard

Measure what you can control.

- Did I do the 3-Word Check today.
- Did I use 4-4-6 before a hard moment.
- Did I move my body for ten minutes.
- Did I set or honor one boundary.
- Did I make one repair quickly.
- Did I connect on purpose with one person.
- Did I sleep within my usual window.

Aim for consistency, not perfection. Five of seven is a winning week.

At-a-Glance Summary

Emotional fitness is noticing, naming, regulating, and responding with your values.
You build it by simple, repeatable tools, 3-Word Check, 4-4-6 breathing, calm kit, movement, boundary sentences, and repair routines.
Use it at school, work, and home with short scripts and small actions.
Protect it by curating inputs, respecting sleep, and choosing nourishing routines.
Measure it by consistency and faster recovery, not by never feeling big emotions.

Action Steps You Can Start Today

1. Write your **two boundary sentences** and practice them aloud.
2. Do the **3-Word Check** three times today.
3. Build your **calm kit** and save it as a note on your phone.
4. Send one **encouragement text** and schedule one **life admin block** this week.
5. Choose one item for your **scorecard** and hit it five days in a row.

You do not need to control every feeling to live well. You need a few honest tools, used often. Emotional fitness grows like any other strength, with practice and time. Train it, and you will carry yourself with steadiness through exams, job searches, conflicts, and changes. That steadiness will spill over into your physical and mental fitness, and together they will shape a life you are proud to live.

Favorite Points and Notes

Physical Fitness

Building Strength and Balance for Life

What does it really mean to be fit? Not just in the "gym selfie" kind of way, but truly fit — in strength, in energy, in spirit. Physical fitness isn't about how you look in the mirror; it's about how you feel when you wake up in the morning, how much energy you have throughout the day, and how capable you feel in your own body.

We live in a world that moves faster every year, yet people are moving *less* than ever. Technology has made life easier in so many ways, but it's also made us still. Many of us spend our days sitting at desks, behind screens, or in cars, scrolling through life instead of living it. The result? Tiredness, stiffness, and a body that feels older than it should. But it doesn't have to be that way.

Physical fitness is a lifelong relationship with your body — a balance of movement, nourishment, and rest. It's about giving your body the care and attention it deserves so it can carry you wherever you want to go in life. Let's talk about how to build that balance, step by step.

The Sedentary Trap: Why Movement Matters More Than Ever

The truth is, we've become a world of sedentary people. Many jobs, schools, and even hobbies revolve around sitting. We sit to work, to study, to drive, to eat, and to relax. It's easy to go through an entire day barely moving at all — and over time, that inactivity takes a toll.

Your body was designed to move. When you don't use it, you lose it — flexibility fades, muscles weaken, circulation slows, and energy levels drop. Even mood and focus decline when your body stays still too long. The opposite is also true: movement heals. Exercise sends oxygen through your blood, boosts endorphins that improve mood, and keeps your heart strong.

If you want to live with energy, mental clarity, and strength, you have to make movement part of your life. It doesn't have to be complicated, expensive, or extreme — it just has to be consistent.

Understanding Physical Fitness

Physical fitness isn't about perfection or competition. It's about building the kind of body that supports the life you want. The American Heart Association and the American College of Sports Medicine recommend at least **150 minutes of moderate-intensity activity each week** (like brisk walking, cycling, or swimming) or **75 minutes of vigorous activity** (like running or high-intensity training), plus **strength training for all major muscle groups at least twice a week.**

That's roughly 30 minutes a day, five days a week — and it can completely change your life.

To truly understand fitness, let's look at its five main components:

1. **Aerobic Fitness** – Your heart, lungs, and blood vessels working together to deliver oxygen during activity.
2. **Muscular Strength** – How much force your muscles can exert.
3. **Muscular Endurance** – How long your muscles can perform repeated contractions before tiring.
4. **Flexibility** – How freely your joints move through their full range of motion.
5. **Body Composition** – The balance of fat, muscle, bone, and water in your body.

When you build all five, you're not just fit — you're resilient, capable, and full of energy for the life you're building.

Movement Is Medicine

Your body is your lifelong home. It's not meant to be punished with exercise — it's meant to be cared for through it. Movement truly is medicine, and the prescription is simple: do something every day that gets your heart beating and your body moving.

You don't have to run marathons or lift heavy weights to stay healthy. Small, consistent actions matter most. Walking your dog briskly, doing bodyweight squats during commercials, parking a little farther from the store, or taking the stairs instead of the elevator all count.

Here's how movement changes your life:

- It increases energy and reduces fatigue.
- It lowers stress and anxiety by releasing endorphins.
- It helps you sleep better.
- It improves posture and confidence.
- It strengthens your immune system.

In short, moving your body regularly makes every other part of your life easier and better.

Building a Realistic Routine

Let's talk about what that looks like in real life. You don't have to be perfect — you just have to begin. Here are examples of daily and weekly movement plans that fit different lifestyles.

If you're a student or have a busy schedule:

- **Monday:** 30-minute brisk walk before class or after dinner

- **Tuesday:** 20 minutes of bodyweight strength (push-ups, lunges, planks)
- **Wednesday:** Yoga or stretching session for flexibility (15–20 minutes)
- **Thursday:** 30 minutes of biking, jogging, or a fitness class
- **Friday:** Full-body strength training or resistance bands
- **Weekend:** Fun movement — hiking, swimming, playing a sport, or just exploring outdoors

If you work full-time:

- Use your breaks to move — 10 minutes of walking after lunch, or 5 minutes of stretching every hour.
- Try "micro-workouts": quick bursts like squats, jumping jacks, or planks throughout the day.
- Schedule a 30-minute walk or light jog before or after work — think of it as your daily reset.

If you prefer home workouts:
You don't need a gym to be fit. A yoga mat, a couple of dumbbells, or even a sturdy chair can help you build strength.

- **Example 20-Minute Circuit (repeat 3x):**
    - 10 squats
    - 10 push-ups (knees or full)
    - 20 jumping jacks
    - 10 lunges (each leg)
    - 20-second plank
    - 10 sit-ups

Remember: The goal is progress, not perfection. A missed workout doesn't undo your effort. What matters is showing up again tomorrow.

Strength: Building the Foundation

Strength training is one of the most powerful ways to transform your body — and your confidence. When you build muscle, you improve your posture, metabolism, and overall function. Lifting isn't just about "bulking up." It's about being strong enough to carry groceries, move furniture, or chase your kids someday without injury.

You can build strength using your own body weight, resistance bands, dumbbells, or machines. The key is to challenge your muscles a little more each time. Aim to work all major muscle groups — legs, back, chest, arms, shoulders, and core — at least twice a week.

If you're new to it, start simple:

- **Bodyweight Squats:** Strengthen your legs and glutes.
- **Push-ups:** Build upper body and core strength.
- **Lunges:** Improve balance and stability.
- **Planks:** Strengthen your entire core.
- **Rows or Band Pulls:** Build back and shoulder strength.

You don't have to lift heavy to get results. What matters is form, consistency, and effort.

Endurance: Training for Stamina and Longevity

Endurance training builds more than physical capacity — it builds mental toughness. It's what allows you to push through challenges, both in workouts and in life. You can develop endurance with any sustained activity that raises your heart rate: walking, swimming, cycling, running, or dancing.

Start where you are. If you're out of shape, even 10 minutes of walking is a great start. Add a few minutes each week until you reach the 30-minute mark. Consistency will improve your stamina faster than you think.

If you like structure, here's a sample week:

- **Day 1:** 30 minutes of brisk walking
- **Day 2:** Rest or light stretching
- **Day 3:** 20 minutes of jogging or cycling
- **Day 4:** Strength training
- **Day 5:** 30-minute walk or dance workout
- **Weekend:** Active fun — sports, yard work, or a long outdoor walk

The point isn't just to exercise, but to build a *lifestyle* of movement.

Flexibility: Staying Loose and Balanced

Flexibility doesn't get the attention it deserves. It's what keeps you moving comfortably, prevents injuries, and supports every other area of fitness. When your muscles are tight, even simple activities like bending or reaching can strain your body.

Try to stretch a little each day, even for 5–10 minutes. Focus on your neck, shoulders, back, hips, and legs — the areas that tighten most from sitting. Yoga, Pilates, or just gentle stretching before bed can make a world of difference.

A few easy options:

- Shoulder rolls and chest stretches to combat screen posture
- Hamstring and hip stretches after long periods of sitting
- Gentle spinal twists for mobility
- Deep breathing while stretching to relax both body and mind

Being flexible isn't about touching your toes — it's about moving through life without pain.

Fueling Your Body: Nutritional Fitness

Now that we've talked about movement, let's shift to something just as important — how you *fuel* your body. You can work out for hours, but if you're eating junk, your body can't perform at its best. Fitness isn't only what you do with your body; it's also what you put into it.

Think of food as fuel, not filler. Everything you eat either helps or harms your energy, focus, and performance. Nutritional fitness means choosing foods that work *with* your body — whole, natural, plant-based foods that nourish and energize you.

Your body needs three main nutrients called **macronutrients**:

- **Carbohydrates** for energy
- **Proteins** for building and repairing muscles
- **Fats** for hormone balance and long-term energy

And it needs **micronutrients** — vitamins and minerals — to keep your heart, brain, and immune system working properly. When you eat real food, you get all of these naturally. When you eat processed food, you get calories without the nutrients your body truly needs.

The Power of Whole Foods

Whole foods are foods that are close to their natural state. They haven't been stripped of nutrients or stuffed with additives. Think of foods that grew from the ground, swam in the sea, or came from the earth — fruits, vegetables, whole grains, beans, nuts, and lean proteins.

When you eat this way, your body rewards you with energy, focus, and strength. You'll recover faster after workouts, sleep better, and even think more clearly.

Here are some examples of healthy, balanced meals that focus on whole, plant-based foods:

Breakfast Ideas:

- Oatmeal topped with fresh fruit, nuts, and a drizzle of honey
- Smoothie made with spinach, banana, berries, chia seeds, and almond milk
- Whole grain toast with avocado and a sprinkle of salt, pepper, and lemon

Lunch Ideas:

- Quinoa or brown rice bowl with black beans, corn, salsa, and grilled vegetables
- Mixed greens salad with chickpeas, tomatoes, cucumbers, olive oil, and balsamic vinegar
- Lentil soup with whole grain crackers or fruit on the side

Dinner Ideas:

- Grilled salmon, roasted sweet potatoes, and steamed broccoli
- Stir-fried tofu with mixed vegetables over brown rice
- Whole grain pasta with sautéed spinach, mushrooms, and a touch of olive oil and garlic

Snacks:

- Apple slices with peanut butter
- Handful of almonds or walnuts
- Carrot sticks and hummus
- Greek yogurt with berries

Hydration:
Water is essential. Most people are slightly dehydrated and don't realize it. Aim for at least **half your body weight in ounces** each day — more if you're active. Skip sugary sodas and energy drinks; they give short bursts followed by crashes.

If plain water gets boring, add lemon slices, cucumber, or mint for natural flavor.

Fuel Before and After Exercise

What you eat before and after workouts matters.

Before you move:

- Eat something with carbohydrates and a little protein.
    - Examples: a banana and handful of nuts, oatmeal with fruit, or a smoothie.

After you move:

- Focus on protein and hydration to help your muscles recover.
    - Examples: a protein smoothie, eggs and whole grain toast, or a rice-and-bean bowl.

Think of your meals as part of your training. The right food helps you perform, recover, and grow stronger.

Rest, Recovery, and Balance

Fitness doesn't come from the gym alone — it comes from recovery too. Rest is where your body rebuilds and strengthens itself. Without it, your progress slows and burnout begins.

Sleep at least **7 to 9 hours per night.** When you don't rest enough, your hormones fall out of balance, your focus fades, and your body starts craving junk food for quick energy. Sleep is as essential to fitness as exercise itself.

Also, listen to your body. Rest days aren't lazy days — they're smart days. If your muscles are sore, stretch instead of lifting. Take a walk, do yoga, or just breathe deeply. Recovery keeps you strong and prevents injury.

Avoiding Extremes

The fitness world can be noisy. There's always a new trend, a "perfect" diet, or a challenge that promises fast results. But physical fitness isn't about extremes — it's about balance and sustainability.

Working out too hard or dieting too strictly can do more harm than good. You don't have to count every calorie or punish yourself for missing a workout. Progress happens through consistency, not perfection.

Remember, fitness should *add* joy to your life — not take it away. Move because you love your body, not because you're trying to earn your worth. Eat because food fuels your dreams, not your guilt.

Staying Active in a Busy World

Life will always be busy. The secret is learning how to move through your days with intention.

Here are a few simple ways to stay active when life feels full:

- Walk or bike to nearby places instead of driving.
- Take the stairs when possible.
- Stretch while watching TV.
- Do squats while brushing your teeth or planks while scrolling social media.

- Get a standing desk or take "walk breaks" every hour at work.
- Make active plans with friends — hiking, kayaking, dancing, or playing a sport.

The goal isn't to exercise once in a while. It's to live an active life.

Motivation and Mindset

There will be days you won't feel like moving. That's normal. Motivation fades, but discipline carries you through. Think about your "why." Maybe you want more energy, more confidence, or a longer, healthier life. Whatever it is, hold onto it.

Set goals you can reach — small wins lead to big success. Maybe your first goal is walking three times a week, drinking more water, or doing ten push-ups. Celebrate every bit of progress.

Fitness isn't about what happens in a week — it's about what happens over years. Build habits that you can live with.

The Payoff: Why It All Matters

When you move your body, feed it well, and give it rest, you feel the difference. You stand taller, breathe easier, and think clearer. Physical fitness gives you energy to chase your dreams, confidence to face challenges, and strength to care for the people you love.

And here's the truth: when you take care of your body, you're taking care of your mind too. Exercise reduces stress, improves mood, and even boosts focus and creativity. It's all connected — body, mind, and spirit.

Physical Fitness: Building Strength and Balance for Life – At-a-Glance Summary

Your body is your lifelong home.
Treat it with care, movement, and respect. Physical fitness isn't about perfection or appearance; it's about building strength, energy, and balance so you can live fully and confidently at every stage of life.

The Basics of Physical Fitness

- **Move regularly.** Aim for **150 minutes of moderate activity** (like brisk walking or cycling) or **75 minutes of vigorous activity** (like running or high-intensity training) each week.
- **Strength train twice weekly.** Work all major muscle groups to build lean muscle and protect your joints.
- **Stretch daily.** Improve flexibility and prevent injury with short stretching or yoga sessions.
- **Rest well.** Sleep 7–9 hours each night and take rest days so your body can recover and rebuild.

Key Components of Fitness

1. **Aerobic Fitness:** Improves endurance and heart health.
2. **Muscular Strength:** Builds power and confidence.
3. **Muscular Endurance:** Trains your body to keep going under stress.
4. **Flexibility:** Keeps your body loose, balanced, and injury-free.
5. **Body Composition:** Maintain a healthy balance of muscle, fat, and hydration.

Daily Movement Ideas

- Walk or bike instead of driving short distances.
- Take a 10-minute walk after meals.
- Stretch while watching TV or during study breaks.
- Do bodyweight exercises — squats, planks, lunges, or push-ups — at home.
- Dance, swim, hike, or play a sport you enjoy.

The goal isn't perfection. It's *consistency*. Move your body every day in ways that feel natural and rewarding.

Fueling Your Body

- **Eat real food.** Focus on fruits, vegetables, whole grains, beans, nuts, and lean proteins.
- **Limit processed foods.** Avoid excess sugar, refined carbs, and artificial ingredients.
- **Hydrate.** Drink water throughout the day; aim for half your body weight in ounces.
- **Fuel before and after workouts.**
    - Before: light carbs + protein (banana, oatmeal, smoothie).
    - After: protein-rich meals (eggs, yogurt, rice and beans, or lean fish).

Healthy Meal Examples

- **Breakfast:** Oatmeal with fruit and nuts or avocado toast on whole grain bread.
- **Lunch:** Quinoa bowl with vegetables and chickpeas.
- **Dinner:** Grilled salmon or tofu with sweet potatoes and steamed broccoli.
- **Snacks:** Apples with peanut butter, almonds, hummus and veggies, or Greek yogurt with berries.

Rest, Recovery, and Mindset

- Rest is part of the plan, not a break from it.
- Listen to your body — stretch when sore, sleep when tired.
- Avoid extremes. Fitness should bring joy, not stress.
- Progress, not perfection, is the key.
- Remember your "why." You're investing in your future self.

Quick Takeaway

Physical fitness builds confidence, energy, and resilience.
Move with purpose, eat with awareness, and rest with intention. Your body responds to consistency, not perfection.

Strong body, balanced mind, fulfilled life — that's real fitness.

Final Thought:
Your physical fitness is a reflection of self-respect. It's your promise to yourself that you will show up — not perfectly, but consistently. You don't have to be the fastest, the strongest, or the fittest. You just have to keep moving forward.

Your body is capable of amazing things. Treat it like the gift it is, and it will carry you confidently through every chapter of your life.

Favorite Points and Notes

Chapter Five

Faith

Faith

The Quiet Power

You Carry Every Day

"Faith is the strength by which a shattered world shall emerge into the light."~ Helen Keller

This chapter is not about religion. It is not about being Christian, Jewish, agnostic, atheist or any one of the thousands of religions in the world. It is about faith, your faith, the trust that lives in your heart and soul. Your religion, if you have one, may shape how you practice your faith and beliefs, how you worship, or how you seek meaning. Even if you do not identify with a religion at all, you still live with faith, because faith is the quiet confidence that there is purpose in your life, that your choices matter, that your next step counts even when you cannot see ten steps ahead.

I want to talk to you, personally and directly, about the kind of faith that gets you through ordinary Tuesdays and unexpected storms. The kind of faith that steadies your hands during exams, breakups, job interviews, and late rent. The kind of faith that whispers, you can do the next right thing, when your mind is loud and your courage is small.

Faith and Hope, Partners but Not The Same

People often mix up faith and hope. They belong together, yet they are not the same. Hope looks forward with desire. Faith stands firm in the present. Hope says, I want a specific outcome. Faith says, I trust while I act. You can hope to get the job, but faith is what makes you prepare thoughtful questions, practice your answers, show up on time, and follow up with gratitude even if the answer is no.

Think of it like this.

- **Faith is trust.**
- **Hope is wishing.**
- **Faith is patience.**
- **Hope is anticipation.**
- **Faith says, the right answers will come.**
- **Hope says, I want this specific answer.**

A farmer plants seeds in a drought. That is faith, acting now. The farmer looks to the sky and longs for rain. That is hope, looking ahead. Both matter. Faith puts your hands to work. Hope lifts your eyes to the horizon. You need both to grow.

Mini-Exercise: Separate Faith from Hope

Write two short lists.
List A, what you are doing this week to move your life forward. List B, what you are wishing for. Circle one item on List B and write one action you can take today that aligns with it. Turn a wish into stepping out on faith to make it happen.

Why Faith Matters Right Now

Look around. The world is noisy. News cycles amplify fear. Friends disagree and forget to be kind. There are wars, crimes, and unrest you cannot control. You might ask, what difference does my small faith make. Here is the answer. Faith is the difference between reacting and responding, between panic and presence. Faith is not a magic escape. It is a steady posture. Faith says, I will meet reality as it is, and I will still choose purpose, love, and integrity.

Both fear and faith ask you to believe in what you cannot see. What you choose, how you respond determines your future. One writes a story of hiding. The other writes a story of growth. You will always have evidence for either or both. Choose your response wisely.

What Faith Does For You

- Lowers stress by calming your inner narrative, you are not alone, you can handle the next step.
- Builds courage by helping you act even when you feel afraid.
- Grows optimism by teaching you to look for options, not just obstacles.
- Strengthens relationships by calling out the best in people and setting compassionate boundaries.
- Anchors purpose by connecting your daily choices to a larger story.
- Transforms mistakes into lessons rather than scars you hide.

Micro-Practice: The 90-Second Reset

When overwhelming feelings spike, set a 90-second timer. Deeply inhale for four, hold for four, exhale for six. Repeat. Whisper, just do the next right thing. Then do it. This is faith in motion.

Faith, Science, and the Space Beyond Measurement

I believe in science. You should too. Observation, measurement, and experiments all keep airplanes in the sky, they keep water clean, and they keep surgeons prepared. Yet not every essential part of human life fits in an experiment or on a chart. Love is not a lab calculation. Meaning is not on a spreadsheet. Courage cannot be weighed on a scale. But they can all be felt and have evidence of being real. This is where faith lives, in the space where data runs out and values must lead.

Let science do what science does, and let faith do what faith does. You do not need to force them into the same box. You can respect both, learn from both, and let both shape a full, grounded life. Some of our greatest Scientists were not only full of wonder, they were full of faith as well.

Reflection Prompt

Where do you rely on proof, and where do you rely on trust. Ponder each for a few minutes. Notice that both show up every day. Notice how they both have a role in your life.

Faith Already Shows Up in Your Day

You trust a chair to hold you when you sit down. You trust a traffic light to stop on-coming cars. You trust your phone alarm to ring and wake you and your friend to understand your text. Does it always happen? No, but you are living out your faith without naming it. The question is not whether you have faith, it is whether you will consciously apply it to the parts of life that matter most, your growth, your relationships, your contributions, your future.

Faith is not about winning. It is not a scoreboard. Faith is about peace regardless of the outcome. It is about showing up fully, doing the work you can do, and staying kind and courageous even when the results are different from what you wanted.

Faith In People

Having faith in people is not the same as being naive. It means you watch patterns, keep your boundaries, and still choose to look for potential. It sounds like this, I believe you can do hard things, so I will not rescue you from growth. I believe you can learn, so I will give you honest feedback. I believe you can change, so I will notice your effort, not just your outcomes.

Simple Script You Can Use

- To a friend, I see how hard you are trying, and I believe you can finish this, what is one step you can take today.
- To a teammate, You are capable of this responsibility, let's break the task into two smaller wins and get you moving.
- To yourself, I can grow into this, I do not need to be perfect, I will take the first step and learn from it.

Exercise: The Encouragement Text

Open your messages and send one person a thoughtful, specific note about their effort, not their talent. Example, I noticed you studied even when you were tired, that is real grit, keep going. Your faith in them becomes a mirror.

Faith In Yourself

It is often harder to believe in yourself than to believe in others. You know your doubts, your past mistakes, your quiet insecurities. Self-faith is not arrogance. It is humble confidence. It sounds like, I am still learning, I do not know everything yet, but I am on a path that matters, and I can keep going.

I believe people can grow. I believe they can learn, heal, build, rebuild, and begin again. Not everyone will. Some will stay stuck in their mire forever. Some will rise only to their comfort level. Some will rise only to their self-imposed limiting beliefs. But some, some will rise farther than they ever imagined. Their faith is the part of them that lifts them beyond conventional wisdom and expectations.

Build Self-Faith With Evidence

Create a running list called Proof I Can Trust Myself. Add small wins daily. I kept my word, I sent the email, I asked for help, I went for a walk, I studied for thirty minutes. Your brain learns from repetition. Give it proof.

The One-Riser Rule

When your mind insists on seeing the whole staircase, shrink your horizon. You only need the next riser. Apply, ask, write one paragraph, clean one drawer, drink one glass of water, take one walk around the block. Small kept promises create momentum, momentum builds faith. Remember Martin Luther King Jr. said "Faith is taking the first step even when you don't see the whole staircase".

Exercise: Three Witnesses

Ask three people who know you, What strengths do you see in me that I forget. Write their words on a note in your phone. Read that note before hard tasks. Borrow belief from others until yours grows stronger and you can see them for yourself.

Faith Versus Fear

Fear is loud. It will show you vivid worst-case scenes and call them wisdom. Faith is steady. It will show you the next honest action. Here is how to move from fear to faith when your stomach drops. Remember, fear is a reaction, courage is a decision and you must have faith to have courage.

1. **Name it.** Say the fear in plain language. Naming shrinks it.
2. **Right-size it.** Ask, what is the most likely outcome, not the scariest.
3. **Regulate your body.** Breathe slowly, drink water, take a five-minute walk.

4. **Share the load.** Tell one trusted person, let them walk beside you.
5. **Return to your creed.** Repeat two sentences that anchor you.

Create Your Two-Sentence Creed

Write two sentences that state who you are and how you respond under pressure. Example, I tell the truth and I keep my word, I choose courage over comfort and take the next right step. Put it where you can see it.

When Faith Feels Far Away

Everyone goes through seasons when faith dips. You might think, if I had prayed more, believed harder, tried longer, the outcome would be different. You may feel disappointment and wonder where faith is when you do not get the answer you wanted. Faith can move in waves, much like grief. It does not mean your faith failed. It means life took a different turn and surprised you; your feelings are still catching up. You may question the outcome, but there is an answer. You just may not know the answer or understand the answer yet.

Here is an example: A dear friend of mine was very sick. Family, friends, church family, coworkers all prayed for healing. Their faith was strong, and they were steadfast in their beliefs. And then, my friend passed away. Does that mean that faith failed? No, it means there was another plan that we could not see. It means we stay in faith and trust that even in tragic circumstances, God uses those to achieve a greater purpose.

Acceptance becomes a shelter. Acceptance is not giving up. It is stopping the fight with reality, so you can fully engage your choices. A timeless reflection says, give me serenity to accept what I cannot change, courage to change what I can, and wisdom to know the difference. Read that slowly. Acceptance, courage, wisdom. Those three words can guide you through almost anything.

Exercise: The Circle of Control

Draw two circles. Inner circle, what I can control. Outer circle, what I cannot. Fill them in for a current challenge. Commit to act only inside the inner circle this week. That choice frees energy and restores faith.

Rebuilding Faith After a Hit

Sometimes your faith gets shaken, a betrayal, a layoff, a breakup, a failure, a scary diagnosis, a death. You may feel cynical, distant, or numb. Rebuilding faith is possible. It is also gradual.

1. **Acknowledge the loss.** Write what happened and how it affected your trust. Be specific, no sugarcoating.
2. **Name the lesson.** What will you do differently to protect your peace going forward. Boundaries, due diligence, pacing, clearer expectations.
3. **Start with tiny signals.** Keep one small daily promise. Prove to yourself that your faith can be visible in small things.
4. **Practice guarded openness.** You can be kind and wise at the same time. Open the door a little, not all the way.
5. **Invite accountability.** Ask a mentor or friend to check in on you. External support strengthens your internal resolve.

Example Scenarios

- **After a breakup.** You rebuild faith by honoring a no-contact window, doing the things you avoided, scheduling movement, reconnecting with friends,

and writing a list of qualities you will require in future relationships.
- **After being laid off.** You rebuild faith by finishing your resume, asking for two referrals each week, applying to a set number of roles, and taking a short course to sharpen skills.
- **After failing a class.** You rebuild faith by meeting the professor, mapping the retake, setting a daily study block, and getting an accountability partner.
- **After a death.** Give yourself grace. Give yourself time to grieve. There is no right time limit. Be gentle with yourself and remember you were given a gift of loving someone so much that you feel the loss and ache of their absence. Your faith will give you the strength to keep moving.

Training Your Faith Like a Muscle

Faith grows with practice. Think of it as training your inner core. You do not need a perfect plan. You need simple, repeatable habits.

Daily Habits That Build Faith

- **Curate your inputs.** Your mind becomes what it consumes. Follow people who teach and elevate, not outrage. Read a few pages of a solid book. Take breaks from noise.
- **Reflect in writing.** Capture three lines each night, what mattered, what you learned, what you will try tomorrow. Reflection turns experience into wisdom.
- **Move your body.** Movement is a physical vote for life. Walk, stretch, lift, breathe. Sleep is also a faith practice, your body needs to repair.
- **Keep tiny promises.** Two non-negotiables daily. Water when you wake up, ten minutes of tidy, five minutes of prayer or quiet, a quick text of encouragement.

- **Serve.** Help one person without keeping score. Service grows perspective.
- **Speak your values aloud.** Your words shape your posture. Rehearse your creed.
- **Pair hope with action.** Keep your eyes open for possibilities, and keep your hands on today's work.

Weekly Habits That Reinforce Faith

- **One scared-but-honest action.** Make the call, ask the question, request feedback.
- **One digital sabbath period.** A half day with your phone on do not disturb.
- **One long walk or workout.** Move long enough to clear your mind.
- **One hour of skill practice.** Invest in your future self.
- **One hour of relationship maintenance.** Family, friends, mentors.

A 30-Day Faith Builder Plan

You can use this as a blueprint. Adjust the timing to your real life.

Week 1, Awareness and Inputs

- Write your two-sentence creed.
- Do the Circle of Control for one problem.
- Unfollow five accounts that inflame rather than inform.
- Keep two tiny daily promises, water on waking, ten minutes of tidy.
- Journal three lines each night.

Week 2, Action and Accountability

- Choose one meaningful goal for the month, job search, class improvement, fitness baseline, and define two weekly actions.
- Tell one person your goal and schedule a check-in.
- Do one scared-but-honest action.
- Send two encouragement texts.
- Keep your two tiny daily promises.

Week 3, Boundaries and Rest

- Plan one digital sabbath window.
- Write, in clear language, one boundary you need, and practice saying it aloud.
- Take one long walk or workout.
- Review your tiny promises and add a third, five minutes of quiet or prayer.
- Journal a short reflection, what changed in my stress this week.

Week 4, Contribution and Reflection

- Serve one person with a concrete act, tutoring, ride, resume review, a meal.
- Do one hour of skill practice for your future self.
- List five lessons you learned this month.
- Write a short letter to yourself, I am proud that you, I noticed that you, keep going because.
- Choose one habit from this month to keep for the next ninety days.

Faith at School, Work, and Home

At School

Faith looks like showing up for office hours, asking the question you are afraid to ask, spreading out your study over days, and resting the night before. It looks like forgiving yourself for a rough test and using it as a roadmap. It looks like joining a study group and inviting quiet classmates into the conversation. It looks like setting boundaries with a friend who distracts you and kindly saying, I want to hang out, but I need to study first.

At Work

Faith looks like preparing for meetings, doing your follow-up quickly, owning your mistakes, and learning fast. It looks like asking for feedback, yes, even the tough kind. It looks like setting a clear start and stop time for your day so you do not burn out. It looks like advocating for your ideas with humility. It looks like noticing a teammate's effort and saying so.

At Home

Faith looks like having the hard conversation instead of avoiding it. It looks like doing your part without keeping score. It looks like saying please and thank you. It looks like resting when your body says rest, cooking a simple meal, cleaning your space, honoring your budget, and planning for the week on Sunday night so you can breathe on Monday morning.

Faith and Boundaries

Faith does not mean letting people walk over you. Faith and boundaries are friends. Faith says, I believe the best in you, and I will protect the space I need to be healthy. Boundaries are not punishments. They are clear lines that keep love and respect possible.

Boundary Scripts

- I want to support you, I am not able to respond during work hours, I will get back to you at 6.

- I care about you, I am not okay with yelling, we can talk when we are calm.
- I want to help, I cannot loan money, I can help you think through a plan.

Faith and Forgiveness

Forgiveness releases your grip on the past so your hands are free for the present. It does not excuse harm. It does not erase boundaries. Forgiveness is a choice you make for your own peace. Sometimes you forgive daily for a while. That is normal. Pair forgiveness with wisdom. You can forgive and still choose a different level of access.

Exercise: The Letter

Write a letter you will never send. Say everything you would say if you could be perfectly honest, then safely destroy it. You can make it a ritual, set it on fire, tear it up, whatever. Just release the feelings so you can move forward with appropriate boundaries.

Faith and Failure

Failure is not a verdict, it is information. Your faith will grow faster when you treat failure like feedback. Ask three questions, what went well, what would I change, what is the next small step. Then move. Do not wait to feel ready. You become ready by doing.

Five-Minute Post-Failure Routine

1. Breathe, then write the three questions.
2. Call one friend who can listen without fixing.
3. Do one small repair action within twenty-four hours.

Faith and the Body

Your mind, heart, and body are connected. When your body is exhausted, faith feels far away. Treat your body like a partner in your growth. Hydrate early, move daily, eat real food when you can, go to bed close to the same time. A healthy routine is not punishment, it is a kindness to your future self. Energy makes courage easier.

Simple Anchor Routine

- Water when you wake up.
- Three deep breaths before any hard task.
- Ten minutes minimum of movement daily.
- Lights down an hour before bed.

Conversations with Yourself

Your self-talk can be a friend or a critic. Train it. When you catch harsh words, shift to truthful, kind words. Not empty flattery, honest encouragement.

- Instead of, I always mess up, say, I am learning, next time I will try X.
- Instead of, I am not qualified, say, I am growing into this, I can learn one skill this week.
- Instead of, No one believes in me, say, I can find one person to support me, and I can be that person for myself.

Exercise: The Mirror Minute

Once a day, look in the mirror and state one truth, one effort, one intention. Truth, I have come through hard things. Effort, today I will practice for twenty minutes. Intention, I choose courage over comfort.

Community, Mentors, and You

Faith grows in good company. Find people who want the best for you and will tell you the truth. If you cannot find them yet, start by being that person. Encourage others. Share resources. Ask questions. Join clubs, volunteer teams, study groups, or professional associations. Community is not a luxury, it is a lifeline. Strong circles carry you farther than lone-wolf grit.

Mentor Email Template

Subject, Student interested in learning from your experience Body, Hello, my name is ___, I admire your work in ___, would you be open to a brief call or coffee so I can ask three questions about getting started in this field, I will come prepared and keep to twenty minutes, thank you for considering.

Measuring Faith Differently

Results matter, yet they do not tell the whole story. Do not measure your faith only by wins. Measure it by presence and integrity.

- Did you show up fully.
- Did you act with honesty.
- Did you keep your word.
- Did you learn and adjust.
- Did you rest when you needed to.
- Did you remain kind, to yourself and to others.

Those are the metrics that build a life you are proud to live.

A Personal Word About Choosing Faith

There were seasons when my own faith flickered, in God, in people, in myself. I fell down. I stood up again. I chose to keep choosing faith. I chose it because every great bridge was once only a sketch, every cure was once only a hunch, every masterpiece was once only a blank page, every comeback was once only a decision. Someone trusted before there was proof. Someone walked before the map was clear. You can be that someone for your own life.

Choose one place to place your faith today. Choose one person to believe in. Choose one value to act on. Choose one step when you cannot see step ten. Your life does not need perfect certainty. It needs practiced courage. Faith gives you that courage.

Your Two-Minute Creed

- I tell the truth and keep my word.
- I choose courage over comfort.
- I take the next honest step.
- I respect science and cherish mystery.
- I believe people can grow, including me.
- I forgive freely and set wise boundaries.
- I do small things consistently.
- I plant seeds in droughts.
- I trust that meaning can grow from pain.

At-a-Glance Summary

Faith is your grounded trust in the present that moves your hands and feet, while hope looks forward. You need both.

Faith does steady your mind, lower stress, build courage, strengthen relationships, anchor purpose, and turn failures into lessons.

Faith looks like small kept promises, honest conversations, boundaries with kindness, showing up for your work, moving your body, resting with intention, and choosing a next step without certainty.

How to practice curate inputs, reflect daily, keep two tiny promises, serve one person, move your body, speak your values, pair hope for tomorrow with action today.

When faith dips accept what you cannot change, act on what you can, practice guarded openness, invite accountability, and rebuild slowly with tiny signals.

Measure faith by presence, integrity, growth, and kindness, not just by wins.

Exercises and Tools

1) The Faith Journal, 5 Minutes Nightly

- Three lines, what mattered, what I learned, what I will try tomorrow.
- Add one win to Proof I Can Trust Myself.

2) The Courage Call

- Once a week, call one person who strengthens you. Share one goal for the week and one step you will take. Ask for a check-in next week.

3) The Boundary Rehearsal

- Write one boundary you need. Practice the sentence three times out loud. Use calm voice, clear words, short sentences.

4) The Seed in a Drought

- Choose one goal with no guaranteed outcome, apply to one stretch role, submit one portfolio piece, ask one mentor, show up to one club. Plant the seed anyway.

5) The 30-Day Plan

- Follow the weekly plan in this chapter. Put each action into your calendar. Treat these appointments with the same respect you give to others.

6) The Mirror Minute

- Truth, effort, intention. One minute daily. Train your inner voice to be honest and kind.

7) The Circle of Control

- Redraw it whenever anxiety spikes. Commit to one inner-circle action today.

Quick Answers to Common Questions

What if I do not feel anything when I try to practice faith.
Practice anyway. Feelings often follow actions. Keep your promises small and repeatable. Movement before motivation.

What if I trusted someone and they hurt me.
Name the harm, set boundaries, seek support, and rebuild slowly. Forgiveness and access are different decisions. Remember forgiveness is not acceptance of the other person's actions. It is for you, not for them.

Can I be scientific and faithful.
Yes. Respect measurable facts, and also honor values and meanings that cannot be weighed. You can hold both without conflict.

How do I know if I am being naive.
Check for patterns. Ask mentors for perspective. Keep your boundaries. Faith does not require you to ignore red flags.

How do I keep faith when results are slow.
Measure inputs, not just outcomes. Track your kept promises, your practice hours, your applications sent, your conversations had. Progress is the seed, results are the harvest.

You do not need the whole map to begin. You need one present moment of trust, repeated across days. That is faith.

Faith in God: A Steady Hand on Your Shoulder

I know I said this chapter is not about God or religion, but I would be remiss without talking about faith in God. He is the ever-guiding force in my life and my faith in God has gotten me through some challenging, difficult and insurmountable events in my life. Without my faith in God, I truly don't know where I'd be today.

There are moments when your own strength is not enough, when your plans fall apart, when your heart is heavy and your mind is loud. This is where faith in God matters. It is the choice to lean on wisdom higher than your own, to trust a love deeper than your feelings, and to rest in a purpose larger than your plans. Faith in God does not cancel your thinking, it completes it. You still study, prepare, work hard, and act with integrity, but you do it knowing you are carried, guided, and seen.

What Faith in God Does in Real Life

1) It gives you identity.
When you believe God made you on purpose, you stop auditioning for worth. You can learn, fail, grow, and still know you are loved. That steady identity makes courage possible.

2) It anchors you in storms.
Life will bring loss, disappointment, and detours. Faith in God does not promise a storm-free life; it promises a secure anchor. You can grieve and still trust. You can question and still stay close.

3) It reshapes your decisions.
When you believe God cares about how you live, your choices shift. Honesty, patience, generosity, and self-control stop being "nice ideas" and become your daily practice. You choose what's right over what's easy.

4) It lifts your perspective.
Faith in God teaches you to look past the instant result and into the long story. You learn to trade short-term relief for long-term character. You plant seeds even when you cannot see the harvest yet.

5) It softens your heart.
Knowing you are forgiven makes it easier to forgive others. Knowing you are loved makes it easier to love people who are difficult. You set wise boundaries, and you also extend real grace.

When Faith Feels Hard

Every honest person faces doubt. Faith in God is not a "perfect feelings" badge, it is a relationship. Relationships grow through questions, time, and trust. If you feel distant, begin again with small, sincere steps. God is not intimidated by your confusion or your silence. Bring both.

Simple Ways to Practice Faith in God

Daily conversation (prayer).
Talk to God like you would to a wise parent or a loyal friend. Short and honest. "Thank you for today. I'm anxious about this meeting. Please guide my words. Help me act with courage and kindness."

Five minutes in Scripture.
Read a short passage each day and ask questions: What does this say about God? What is He trying to tell me? What does this say about my circumstances? What does it say about me? What is one thing I will do today because of this?

Quiet stillness.
Sit for two minutes, breathe slowly, and repeat a short truth: "I have faith. I believe. I am held. I am guided. I will do the next right thing."

Gratitude and confession.
Write two lines at night: one thank-you for where you saw God's goodness, one honest confession where you missed the mark and want to grow tomorrow.

Serve someone.
Love is faith with hands and feet. Help without expecting anything in return. You will feel your faith strengthened as you give.

A Short Prayer You Can Use

"God, thank You for life and breath today. Give me wisdom to choose what is right, courage to do the next honest thing, and love for the people in my life. Guard my mind from fear, steady my steps, and let my work reflect Your goodness. Amen."

When Answers Are Slow

Sometimes you will pray and wait and wait.... and wait. You will ask and not see change. Waiting is not wasted in God's world. Waiting grows roots—patience, humility, and trust. While you wait, keep doing what is faithful and right: show up, tell the truth, serve, rest, and pray again tomorrow. God's timing is rarely our timing. And remember, God is not Santa Claus, if you pray for something and don't see the results you desire, remember the answer may be "no" or maybe just "not yet".

A Gentle Challenge

Give God thirty days of honest effort. Short prayers, short readings, small obedience, steady gratitude, listen to inspiring faith-filled music. At the end of thirty days, look back. Notice the peace, the clearer decisions, the quieter fear. Faith in God does not remove every problem, but it will change the person who faces them—you.

Remember: You are not an accident or an afterthought. You are known, loved, and invited to live with God's steady hand on your shoulder. You are worthy and you are enough, just as you are. Walk forward in that truth, one faithful step at a time. And always remember He is walking beside you, even when you don't know He's there. He is.

Favorite Points and Notes

www.ingramcontent.com/pod-product-compliance
Lightning Source LLC
Chambersburg PA
CBHW071236070526
44583CB00017B/2201